Touring Sydney

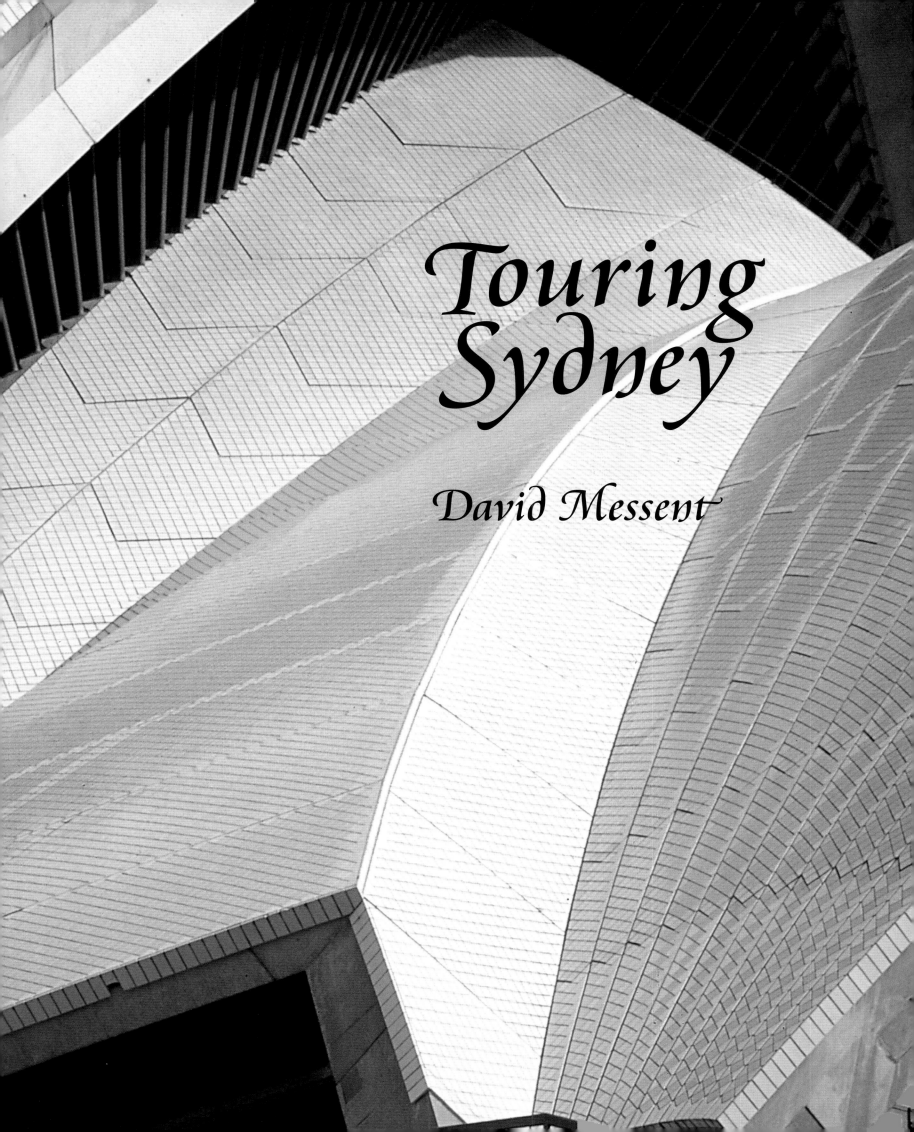

Touring
Sydney

David Messent

This one's for Maryvonne, Jean Michel and the three boys

Produced by
David Messent Photography
Sydney

Published 2000
Revised and updated 2003

Photography	David Messent
Written by	David Messent and Graham White
	The Blue Mountains by Glenda Browne
Design	David Messent and Jill Swart
Helicopter flights	Helicopter Charter
Typesetting and assembly	Max Peatman
Maps	Universal Press

Printed in Singapore by Kyodo

Contents

Sydney City

Fireworks on Sydney Harbour Bridge.

Sydney City

HARBOUR SCENERY AND AUSTRALIAN WILDLIFE

I guess there couldn't be a more logical point to start a tour of Sydney than with the Harbour Bridge. Dominating Sydney's skyline since it was completed in 1932, the Bridge has become an unofficial symbol of Sydney to people all around the world, while its pedestrian footpath and south-east pylon provide a vantage point for spectacular views of the city, Opera House and harbour.

Museum of Contemporary Art

Follow the pavement on the west side of Circular Quay through First Fleet Park to George Street. Turn right on George Street and the first building you reach is the Museum of Contemporary Art. This squat sandstone structure was once the Maritime Services Board building, and maritime motifs decorate the exterior high above the entrance way. The museum is custodian to one of Australia's major collections of modern art, representing the work of over 500 artists from around the world including Henry Moore and Picasso. Included among the works on display are paintings by Dr John Wardell Power whose bequest to Australia for the pursuit of the 'plastic arts' led to the founding of the museum. New exhibitions are frequently displayed in the galleries, often of a rather puzzling nature!

Turn right on George Street outside the museum then left on Argyle Street. Stay on the north pavement of Argyle Street for 200 metres, and ascend Argyle Steps to your right near a concrete bridge over the road. At the top of the steps turn left into Cumberland Street. Bridge Climb just down the road at 5 Cumberland Street is the starting point for an exhilarating three hour adventure climbing to the top of the steel arch of Sydney Harbour Bridge. It really is a terrific thrill to stand 130 metres above the harbour. You are safely buckled to a security cable and escorted all the way by a trained climb leader with a group of 10 other climbers. It's advisable to book ahead if making the climb.

Not quite so exhilarating is to cross the bridge by the pedestrian footway. Bridge Stairs opposite the path where you entered Cumberland Street lead up to the footway.

Shop-fronts on George Street.

The 'Club Med 2' at Sydney Cove Passenger Terminal, Circular Quay.

West Circular Quay bathed in early morning sunshine. The intriguing Museum of Contemporary Art is on the left while the example of contemporary art on the right is the 'Royal Viking Sun'.

Circular Quay and the Sydney skyline. When Governor Phillip arrived in 1788 he chose Sydney Cove from the multitude of bays in the Harbour as the 'one which had the finest spring of water, and in which ships can anchor... close to the shore.'

Sydney from Taronga Zoo.

Sydney Harbour Bridge

The opening ceremony for the Harbour Bridge took place on the roadway just south of the Harbour Bridge pylons on March 19, 1932. The ceremony was turned into a fiasco when an Irishman, Francis de Groot, galloped up on horseback and slashed through the opening ribbon with his sword before the Premier could cut it with a pair of scissors.

De Groot was bundled off his horse, arrested and charged, and at his trial found guilty of offensive behaviour in a public place and of injuring government property... 'to wit one ribbon', and fined £5 with £4 costs.

From the footway you can look down on The Rocks area of Sydney, the first part of Australia settled by Europeans when the First Fleet arrived in 1788; or at least what is left of it; 300 buildings were demolished in The Rocks when the Harbour Bridge and approaches were built. On the Bridge itself a constant stream of traffic passes by. During the rush hour 15,000 vehicles sometimes cross the Bridge every hour, over double the estimated maximum capacity of 6,000 an hour calculated when the Bridge was designed. The two traffic lanes next to the walkway carried trams until 1958, when the lines were pulled up and the new road lanes opened in July 1959.

The Pylon Lookout

The footway soon leads you to the south-east example of one of the 'Pillars of Hercules bestriding the tide', as The Sydney Morning Herald in 1932, dubbed the pairs of pylons gracing both ends of the Bridge. The hollow 89 metre high pylons, constructed from 18,000 cubic metres of granite quarried at Moruya on the south coast of New South Wales, are aesthetic and serve no particular structural purpose. A steel staircase through the inside of the pylon leads up to a display area with photos of the construction of the Bridge and examples of the rivets and steel used in fabrication. An open air observation lookout is right at the top. The pylon is open from 10.00 a.m. to 5.00 p.m., and there is a small entrance charge.

Walk across the Harbour Bridge, through the north west pylon and down the steps to Broughton Street. Hail a cab for the 15 minute journey to Bradleys Head.

Bradleys Head

Three cannons mounted on carriages in gunpits at Bradleys Head are the best preserved example of a series of fortifications that were built on Sydney Harbour headlands during the 1870s.

Bradleys Head, named after Lieutenant William Bradley, a cartographer with the First

Sydney with Bradleys Head in the foreground. Two Manly ferries have just crossed each other on the Harbour.

Fleet who went on to become a Rear Admiral, was the first of Sydney's harbourside military reserves to be handed over for public recreation in 1908.

Descend the steps across the road from the cannons, which take you down to the harbour foreshore, where a ship's mast stands above the remains of some more old gunpits. The mast, from the cruiser *HMAS Sydney*, is a memorial to four men killed in action in the battle of the Cocos Islands on September 9, 1914. During the battle, the first in which a ship of the Royal Australian Navy took part, the Sydney sank the German raider '*Emden*' and captured her crew.

At the end of the car park on Bradleys Head, follow the path past the galvanised steel fence. Continue on the path for about a kilometre, through unspoilt bushland with views on the left across the harbour to the city. The path reaches the road near the lower entrance to Taronga Zoo.

Taronga Zoo

Taronga is aboriginal for 'beautiful view', and I believe that, without question, everyone would agree Taronga Zoo, on its location overlooking Sydney Harbour, is the most beautiful zoo site in the world. Buy a copy of the Taronga Zoo guide and map at the shop near the entrance and search out some of Australia's unique wildlife. Koalas, kangaroos, emus, wombats, the duck-billed platypus and many examples of antipodean birds, reptiles and sea creatures, can all be found. There are also the everyday big cats, apes and bears that help make up Taronga Zoo's total collection of approximately 3,000 marsupials, mammals, birds, reptiles and fish.

The Zoo is open from 9.00 a.m. to 5.00 p.m., although visitors can stay until sunset. As far as it can, the Zoo tries to be self-supporting, and you will notice the names of companies and individuals on many of the cages who sponsor the animals.

The only protection for gunners at Middle Head Fort were these stone trenches.

Exit by the lower entrance to the Zoo and walk down the hill to the wharf at the bottom of the road, from where a regular ferry service runs to Circular Quay. When Taronga Zoo opened in 1916, the animals, including Jessie the elephant, were shipped across the harbour from the old Moore Park Zoo by vehicular ferry and off loaded at the wharf.

A STROLL ON MACQUARIE STREET

Following the struggle to found the colony under Governor Phillip (1788-1792), fresh development was stifled in the first years of the 19th century through the influence of the New South Wales Corps or 'Rum Corps' as they were known, who were able to control the finances of Sydney by using Bengal Rum as a means of exchange, as there was a great

Bronze lion sculptures decorate the entrance of the old Treasury building.

Edward VII looks more like a cavalry captain than a king in this statue in front of the Conservatorium at the top of Bridge Street.

The Justice and Police Museum is housed in the old Water Police Station and Courthouse, in use from 1854 to 1984.

The Conservatorium of Music was designed by convict architect Francis Greenway as stables for Government House.

scarcity of hard currency. An attempt to put the colony's affairs in order when Governor Bligh (of Mutiny on the Bounty fame) was sent out as Governor, ended in disaster in 1808 when the Rum Corps rose and deposed him. So when Brigadier General Lachlan Macquarie arrived in 1810 with his own regiment of Royal Highlanders, though he was able to break the control of the Rum Corps, the administration of Sydney was in a mess or as Macquarie put it:

> … I found the colony barely emerging from infantile imbecility and suffering from various privations and disabilities; the country impenetrable beyond 40 miles from Sydney; agriculture in a yet languishing state; commerce in its early dawn; revenue unknown; threatened by famine; distracted by faction; the public buildings in a state of dilapidation and mouldering to decay; the few roads and bridges formerly constructed, rendered almost impassable; the population depressed by poverty; no public credit nor private confidence; the morals of the great mass of the population in the lowest state of debasement and religious worship almost totally neglected.

During his 12 year term as Governor, ending in 1822, Macquarie certainly transformed Sydney from a state of 'infantile imbecility' into a more respectable colony. His achievements included the erection of over 200 public buildings and the granting of land for Sydney's two cathedrals, setting aside Hyde Park as a public park (1810) and founding the Botanical Gardens (1816), making the colony's first coinage (1813) and opening its first bank, the Bank of New South Wales (1817). He also promoted the first crossing of the Blue Mountains (1813) and founded the new settlements of Richmond, Windsor and Liverpool, on the plains around Sydney. Macquarie could upset people by his autocratic and arrogant style of leadership and his insufferable vanity – he named Macquarie Street after himself and Elizabeth Street after his wife, but there's no diminishing the work he did as Governor.

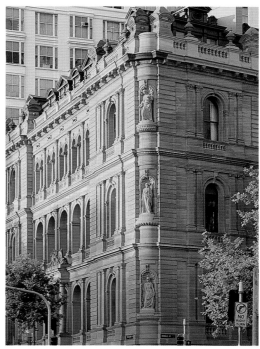

Statues decorate the facade of this grand sandstone structure on Bridge Street which used to house the Colonial Secretary's Office and the department of the Minister for Works.

Justice and Police Museum

At the east end of Circular Quay head up Phillip Street and immediately left on Albert Street. On the corner of Albert and Phillip Streets, occupying the old sandstone Police Station and Courthouse is the Justice and Police Museum. On display is a fascinating array of weaponry taken from criminals over the years, including daggers, guns, hatchets, batons and maces, many used in evidence in murder trials and others used to commit murders which have remained unsolved. Included in the collection are revolvers and pistols captured from the bushrangers Ned Kelly, Ben Hall, Captain Moonlight and Thunderbolt Lightning.

At the end of Albert Street turn right on Macquarie Street past the entrance to the Ritz Carlton Hotel. The hotel, in a former Health Department building, has a foyer, bar and lounge resembling the interior of an English country mansion, with antique furniture, clocks, mirrors, ceramics and cut glass chandeliers.

Continue past a 1938 art deco style building to the Inter-Continental Hotel on the corner of Bridge and Macquarie Streets. If you've left without your breakfast go into the hotel cocktail lounge for a coffee. The lounge is in the courtyard of the former Treasury and Audit Office designed by Colonial Architect Mortimer Lewis and built 1849-51. The first shipments from the Australian gold fields were stored in the Treasury strongroom.

Standing on the opposite corner of Bridge Street is the former Colonial Secretary's Building and the offices of the Minister for Works. Utzon stormed into the Public Works Minister's office on the first floor to tender his resignation as architect of the Sydney Opera House in February 1966. A white marble statue of Queen Victoria adorns the hall inside the main entrance to the Colonial Secretary's Building off Macquarie Street.

The Conservatorium of Music

Continue on Bridge Street past the statue of Edward VII on horseback to the castellated Conservatorium of Music. Free instrument recitals are given by students in the Conservatorium's Concert Hall during term time, check the times given on the noticeboard at the entrance. The Conservatorium was originally the stables for Government House.

You never know who's listening. 'The Huntsman' in the Royal Botanic Gardens.

Designed by Francis Greenway, an architect transported to Australia in 1814, for forging a signature on a building contract, the stables were intended for a palatial Government House that was never built. Commissioner J.T.Bigge, who arrived in Sydney in 1819 to conduct an enquiry into the affairs of the colony, stopped the building of Government House because the design was too costly and criticised Macquarie for making the stable 'such a palace for horses'.

Tropical glasshouses

With the entrance to the Conservatorium of Music at your back, turn left, walk up the grass verge and go through the gate of the Royal Botanic Gardens, then turn right and follow the path.

Continuing on the path through the gardens you soon reach a fountain adorned with bronze statues by the Italian sculptor Simonetti, unveiled during Victoria's Diamond Jubilee Celebration in 1897. Standing tall on the central pedestal is Governor Phillip, clutching a flag in one hand and a proclamation in the other.

Descend the steps in front of Phillip's memorial, pass through the Pioneers Garden and after three or four minutes walk reach the tropical glasshouses. The Arc Glasshouse contains exotic tropical plants, the Pyramid Glasshouse contains Australian tropical plants. There is a small entrance fee. Take the path back towards the city that runs west from the Arc Glasshouse and leave the gardens by the first exit you come to opposite the Public Library.

The State Library

The State Library, Australia's oldest library founded in 1826, contains an excellent reference library and the Mitchell and Dixon collections, between them the greatest collection of Australiana in the world. The Mitchell Library contains such priceless items as Cook's diaries, the log from HMS *Bounty* and eight out of the ten existing journals written by members of the First Fleet (available for viewing on micro-film). Many of these treasures were donated in 1907 when David Scott Mitchell gave his entire collection of 60,000 articles of Australiana to the state. Sir William Dixon, who started collecting when David Scott Mitchell finished, donated his own collection of 20,000 items of Australiana when he died in 1952.

Continue south on Macquarie Street past the modern State Library building, opened in 1988. This is the Macquarie Street Wing of the State Library containing the General Reference Library.

Governor Phillip takes centre stage on this fountain in the gardens.

The Pioneers Garden stands on the site of the Garden Palace, built for the International Exhibition of 1879, which burnt down in a gigantic fire in 1882. The Palace was longer and higher than the Queen Victoria Building in the city.

The Pyramid and Arc glasshouses in the gardens.

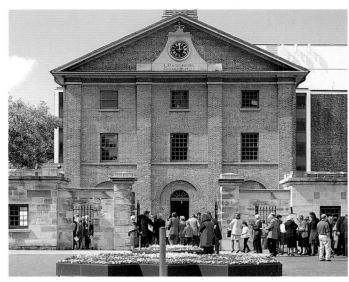

Hyde Park Barracks, 'A Museum about itself', was a barracks for transported convicts.

New South Wales Parliament House.

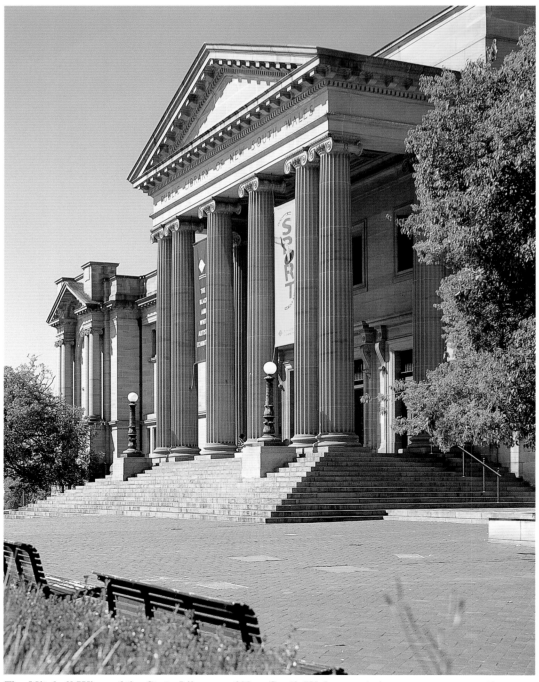

The Mitchell Wing of the State Library of New South Wales, contains, among many other treasures, the Mitchell and Dixon collections, the world's biggest collection of Australiana.

Parliament House

The next building on the left is New South Wales Parliament House. The Georgian style double-storey verandahed building was built in 1811-1816 as the north wing of the 'Rum Hospital' and converted for use by the State Legislative Council in 1829. It is the oldest Parliament in Australia.

Parliament House is open from 9.30 a.m. to 4.00 p.m. on weekdays only. Members of the public are free to walk through the designated areas. Make sure you pick up an interesting little free booklet about Parliament House from the desk at the entrance.

Sydney Hospital

Sydney Hospital, next to Parliament House, occupies the ground where the central wing of the Rum Hospital once stood, demolished in 1880 to make way for the present structure. Behind the main building the Florence Nightingale Wing, opened in 1869 to receive nurses trained by Florence Nightingale, is the oldest part of the hospital.

Macquarie ordered the building of a new hospital in Sydney shortly after his arrival in the colony. The site, on a breezy elevated ridge east of the main town, was apparently the choice of Mrs Macquarie, who also made some sketch plans of the hospital buildings.

The deal Macquarie struck with the triumvirate charged with building the 'Convict Hospital', stipulated '... the said contractors, shall be allowed and have permission to purchase or to import into the colony, the quantity of forty five thousand gallons of spirits... (and) while construction took place... His Excellency will grant no further permission for the importation of spirits...'. In addition the contractors received 20 convict labourers, 20 draught bullocks and 80 oxen for slaughter. At this time the cost price of imported Bengali rum was 3 shillings a gallon which could be retailed in the colony at up to 50 shillings a gallon. The leading partner in the triumvirate carrying out the building work was the acting principal surgeon, D'Arcy Wentworth. Wentworth had previously been suspended by Bligh for alleged misuse of public labour in hospitals, and had supported the insurrection against Bligh.

When the hospital was completed in 1816, it was two feet lower than marked on the plan and Macquarie insisted against the protestations of the contractors that they complete an equivalent amount of labour on other public buildings. The hospital had a high stone wall on the Macquarie Street frontage to prevent convict patients escaping. Patients, who included the city poor as well as convicts, were locked in the wards from evening to sunrise with no toilet facilities. Medicines handed out by convict nurses and wardsmen were often administered to the wrong patient. There was a great shortage of drugs, as orders of medicines requisitioned from England could take up to three years to arrive and if a particular drug for a patient was not available, the next most suitable, in the opinion of the dispenser, was administered.

Concerned at the woeful state of the hospital system, in 1866 Colonial Secretary, Sir Henry Parkes wrote to Florence Nightingale in England for advice. Florence Nightingale replied to Parkes' letter promising her full support, not only for the sake of advancing the cause of medicine but out of a sense of gratitude to the people of Australia for their contributions to the Nightingale Fund immediately following the Crimean War. Nightingale despatched Miss Osburn, with five nursing sisters under her charge trained in her new nursing program, to run Sydney's first training school for probationary nurses to be located at Sydney Hospital. It established a system of nursing that was to endure for a hundred years. The new 'Nightingale Wing' was completed at Sydney Hospital for the use of the school in the 1870s. Miss Osburn remained head of nursing staff until 1884 and maintained a regular correspondence with Florence Nightingale until the latter died.

Tours of the hospital depart at 11.00 a.m. on Wednesdays from the lobby off the main Macquarie Street entrance. Directly past the hospital on the left is the former Mint, located in the south wing of the old Rum Hospital.

Sydney architect Thomas Rowe received the commission to design Sydney Hospital after winning first prize in an architectural competition.

The Nightingale Wing of Sydney Hospital was built to house nursing teachers trained by Florence Nightingale.

The lion and the unicorn on the facade of the Customs House.

St James Church is the oldest in the City of Sydney. Originally designed as a courthouse, the building was converted into a church when the construction of St Andrew's was postponed on the recommendation of Commissioner Bigge.

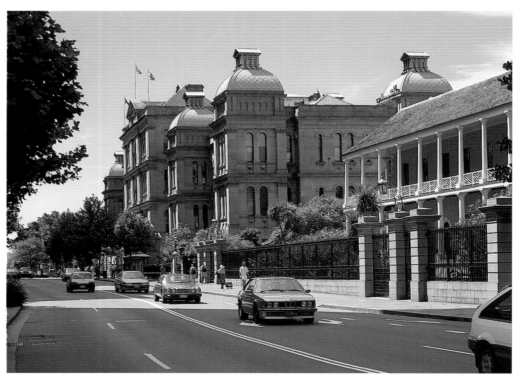

Sydney Hospital and the Mint on Macquarie Street. A critic of Rowe's Sydney Hospital, completed in 1894, wrote that the structure was 'marked by a heavy hand… ponderous, leaden, even dull.'

Australia's first mint once occupied the south wing of Macquarie's 'Rum Hospital'.

Hyde Park Convict Barracks

On the corner of Macquarie Street and Prince Alfred Road stands Hyde Park Barracks Museum. During the early years of the colony, convicts labouring on public works were fed and clothed but not housed and either slept rough or begged for a place to sleep at night. With hundreds of convicts wandering the streets of Sydney every evening after work, crime was rampant. Macquarie had Francis Greenway design and build Hyde Park Convict Barracks (1817-1819), a three storey brick and sandstone dormitory to sleep 600 convicts. Opened on June 4, 1819 by Macquarie, the first 589 convicts staying in the barracks were served 'a most excellent dinner, plum pudding and an allowance of punch'. Following the sumptuous feast the convicts 'cheered His Excellency in reiterated peals'.

Convicts at the Barracks were required to work six days a week from sunrise to sunset, with a stop for lunch. On Sundays at Divine Service 'overseers … will impress on the men the importance of a decorous, attentive and devout demeanour … on Sundays as well as every Thursday, the prisoners put on clean linen… hammocks are properly scrubbed at least once in every quarter, and… the blankets are washed every six months'. As the Chief Engineer wrote in 1819, 'Some (convicts) were pleased and these were the steady and best behaved who looked to it as a place of comfortable lodging and regular diet… there are others of more dissolute dispositions who regarded it as a place of restraint and still regard it as such'.

Being in Hyde Park Barracks was not a punishment in itself, however prisoners were flogged for subsequent offences, the return from the Barracks in 1821 recording that during the year a total of 7,020 lashes were 'inflicted by order of the magistrates'. A convict, William Derrincourt recounted his own flogging at the barracks in the 1820s. '…if a man shouted out through pain he was looked upon as a sandstone or crawler. While the flogger was fixing me up he said to me quietly 'Is there any hangings to it' meaning had I anything to give him to lay the lash lightly. 'Yes' I answered. 'All right' he said and then buckled to his work. The falls of the cat were enough to take my breath away and to draw my blood freely although comparatively lightly laid on…'.

When transportation ended the barracks became a hostel for single immigrant women, a home for old and destitute women, and finally Government departments and courts, before they were restored and reopened in 1984 as a museum. Following its conversion for use by the courts the interior of the Barracks was subdivided into Judges' chambers, rooms for witnesses, records and administration, including a large room for 'lunacy clerks' looking after the paperwork for an adjoining 'Lunacy Court'.

The onion domed clock tower of the Lands Department building on Bridge Street.

Macquarie Place, with the anchor and a cannon from the 'Sirius' on the right. Road distances in New South Wales are measured from Francis Greenway's obelisk on the left.

A statue of Victoria decorates the facade of the old GPO building in Martin Place.

The entry on the west side of the Colonial Secretary's Building.

Statues fill niches on the sides of the Lands Department Building.

St. James Church

Cross Macquarie Street to St. James Church (1819-1822), directly opposite the barracks. St. James was designed originally as a courtroom by Francis Greenway, then Macquarie asked Greenway to change his plans to turn it into a church. Inside the church the fine craftsmanship of the polished marble railing and mosaic floor of the sanctuary make a striking contrast to the relative plainness of the rest of the interior.

Convicts from Hyde Park Barracks were marched across for Sunday service to a separate entrance and gallery of the church with '... their best clothes well brushed, their hands and faces washed and their shoes cleaned'.

Francis Greenway's Supreme Court Building, directly behind the church, still functions as a sheriff's office and has four working courts.

On the forecourt in front of St. James Church near Macquarie Street, go down the steps leading to St James underground station and catch a train one stop to Circular Quay. While you are waiting for your train at St James you will have time to admire the splendour of the station's original 1920's colour scheme of cream and green tiles. General Macarthur had his Sydney wartime headquarters in a disused railway tunnel at the station.

The Museum of Sydney is backed by the massive structure of Governor Phillip Tower.

CENTRAL SYDNEY

Start at Wharf Four at Circular Quay. Sydney Ferries run an excellent information counter on the corner opposite the wharf beneath Circular Quay Station. Just around the corner, opposite the Paragon Hotel, the N.S.W. Government runs a travel centre providing free information on the 'Seven Wonders of New South Wales' and how to get there and where to stay. Cross Alfred Street at the traffic lights to the Customs House, which has the names on scrolls of various outposts of the British Empire decorating the facade.

The interior of the Customs House has recently been transformed into a culinary and cultural venue, with a bar, café, exhibitions and galleries. The program of exhibitions includes the best of Australian and international craft and design. Café Sydney on the fifth floor has a view of Circular Quay and the harbour. The Customs House is open seven days a week from 10 a.m. to 5 p.m. and entry is free.

Macquarie Place

Turn left up Loftus Street to the small park at Macquarie Place, a shady haven not much bigger than the average suburban garden. The park was set aside originally by Governor Macquarie from part of the garden of Old Government House. The flagship of the First Fleet, an old frigate that had served in the American War of Independence and was renamed the *Sirius* for its new mission after the brightest star in the southern sky, sank off Norfolk Island in March 1790 while on a journey to China for supplies. The anchor from the *Sirius* and one of its cannons, recovered in 1907, can be found in the park. A sandstone obelisk nearby, designed by Francis Greenway and erected in 1818, is the benchmark for road distances from Sydney to the rest of Australia.

The clock tower of the old GPO.

Pass the statue of the great Australian pioneer, Thomas Sutcliffe Mort at the south west corner of the park and cross to the Lands Department Building on the corner of Bridge and Gresham Streets. The Lands Department was built over a period of 20 years from the 1870s to the 1890s. A stately onion domed clock tower and an observatory (which was never used) grace the roof. Forty eight niches in the outside walls of the Lands Department contain some statues of Australian explorers and legislators. Twenty five niches were left unfilled when the building was completed, and they have remained vacant ever since. Have there been no explorers or legislators since deemed worthy of occupying the places?

Walk round the exterior of the Lands Department building along Gresham Street, then turn left on Bent Street. The street's irregular course once skirted the vegetable garden of Old Government House.

Cross Farrer Place, ascend the steps and pass through the revolving doors to the foyer of Governor Phillip Tower (1993). The lofty foyer of Governor Phillip Tower and the adjoining Governor Macquarie Tower are like something out of the dying days of the Holy Roman Empire. Walk through the foyer and turn left on Phillip Street to the Museum of Sydney.

Museum of Sydney

The Museum of Sydney stands on the spot where a portable canvas structure carried on one of the First Fleet ships was erected as the first Governor's House. In May 1788

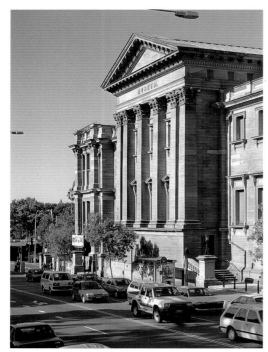

Government Architect James Barnet completed the Australian Museum in 1866 with 'the tympanum of the pediment ... left plain in the hope that at a future day it will be adorned by some emblematic group of sculpture'. However the tympanum has remained bare to this day.

construction commenced on a permanent Government House built in Georgian style from locally made bricks. This building was demolished in 1845, and all that remains are some of the foundations which can be seen through glass panels in the floor of the foyer of the Museum. The most dramatic event to take place at old Government House occurred during the Sydney Rum Rebellion of 1808. The hapless Governor Bligh, who, following the Mutiny on the Botany enjoyed a short term as Governor of N.S.W., was deposed by a mutiny on land during the rebellion. Nearby Bligh Street is named after the Governor. Bligh described in a letter to his friend Joseph Banks how '... This rebellious act was done so suddenly that in about five minutes from the time we first knew of it, Government House was surrounded with troops, Major Johnstone having brought up in battle array above three hundred men under martial law, loaded with ball to attack and seize my person and a few friends... that had been at dinner with me... they marched to the tune of the 'British Grenadiers', and to render the spectacle more terrific to the townspeople, the field artillery... was presented against the house...'.

Martin Place

Back track on Phillip Street into Elizabeth Street and turn right into Martin Place. The banking hall of the Commonwealth Bank at number 48 has a ceiling which is supported by a grove of green marble columns. A white marble lobby, entry and staircase, with a stained glass barrel-vaulted ceiling, opening to the north of the banking hall, is something just wonderful.

Cross Pitt Street to James Barnet's G.P.O. building on the left of Martin Place. When construction of the G.P.O. was commenced in 1866 by Government Architect James Barnet, Australia's postal services had advanced remarkably since the appointment of Australia's first postmaster in 1809. That year Isaac Nichols Esquire; transported for stealing a donkey, started a post office at his own home. The G.P.O. was completed in stages and opened for the colony's centenary in 1887. One of the main attractions for the first users of the Post Office was the opportunity to ride in Sydney's first lifts. The clock wasn't finally fitted to the clock tower until 1891. In 1942 the Sydney Council, concerned that the 64 metre high G.P.O. clock tower may be used as a reference point by Japanese pilots to bomb the centre of Sydney, dismantled the tower and put the pieces in storage. The tower stayed down for over 20 years until it was dusted off and re-erected in 1963.

In Martin Place opposite the G.P.O. on the site where the first recruiting office stood during the First World War, stands the Cenotaph where a dawn service is held every Anzac Day and a memorial service every Remembrance Day at 11.00am on November 11th. Stop for a while to ponder the message 'Lest We Forget', inscribed on the side of the Cenotaph.

The Cenotaph in Martin Place was built on the site of a First World War recruiting office.

The green oasis of Hyde Park in the centre of the city, was set aside as a common by Governor Phillip, 'never to be granted or let lease on'.

Sydney War Memorial and Pool of Remembrance.

Sculptor Raynor Hoff was chosen to execute the sculptures for the War Memorial.

Figures from Greek Mythology on the Archibald Fountain in Hyde Park were the work of Parisian sculptor Francois Sicard.

Raynor Hoff's bas-reliefs on the side of the War Memorial evoke the tragedy and toil of the First World War.

Australia suffered tremendous losses in both World Wars, and casualties in the Malayan Emergency and Vietnam. A memorial service played by members of the 2nd Military District Brass Band takes place at the Cenotaph every Thursday at 12.30 p.m.

Turning right down George Street the High Street of Governor Phillip's Sydney renamed George Street by Governor Macquarie after George III, pass Australia Square Tower on the right. Good views of Sydney can be enjoyed from the revolving Summit Restaurant at the top.

Last but not least; continuing on George Street and under the Cahill Expressway, a minute or so's walk brings you to James Barnet's Rocks Police Station (1882). Note the lion holding a baton in its mouth on the keystone above the entrance. The police station is built on the site of the First Fleet Hospital, a crude structure thrown together from branches, bark and wattle, to house the sick when the First Fleet landed.

HYDE PARK AND PADDINGTON

From Circular Quay, walk up Albert Street and Macquarie Street to Hyde Park. Continue straight on past the Dobell Fountain and cross Park Street to Sydney War Memorial. The building of the Memorial was financed by £60,000 collected from a fund opened on April 25, 1916, the first anniversary of the landing of Australian and New Zealand troops at Gallipoli. Following a design competition the memorial was planned and constructed by Sydney architect Bruce Dellit, with the sculptures the work of Raynor Hoff. Hoff, born in Nottingham, England learnt his basic stone working skills in his father's masonry yard before serving in the trenches in France during the Great War and later moving to Australia, where he taught sculpture at Sydney Technical College.

The Archibald Fountain was bequeathed to the people of Australia in 1932 by J. F. Archibald, publisher of 'The Bulletin' magazine, to commemorate the association of Australia and France in the 1914-18 war.

Dellit felt 'the monument... must be purely contemporary in its style' with the sculptures designed to represent the sacrifice of war, and, 'to give an impression, not of the glory of war, but of its tragedy and horror'.

In Hyde Park north east of the Anzac Memorial is a statue of Captain Cook, erected in 1879, the hundredth anniversary of his death at Owhyhee (Hawaii). Thomas Woolner was commissioned to execute the sculpture, an English sculptor who came to Australia during the gold rush in 1852 but was unsuccessful in his quest for fortune and returned to England in 1854.

Cook's outstretched arm on the statue seems to be gesturing you towards the Australian Museum, directly across the road on College Street.

The Australian Museum

The facade of the Australian Museum facing College Street, was Government Architect James Barnet's first major building completed in the colony. Barnet's original proposal was grander even than the British Museum, built 1837-47. It included a lecture theatre, art gallery, sculpture gallery and library as well as a museum. The main entrance facing William Street was to have had a neo-classical design with a broad flight of steps approaching a columned portico of twelve paired Corinthian columns backed by a large

Paddington terraces were built as working mens' houses in the 1880s and 1890s when Sydney was just a short tram ride away down Oxford Street.

dome. However the only part of Barnet's ambitious scheme to be completed was the present day west wing facing College Street.

The Museum was opened to the public in 1868, with displays of animals, fish, insects and minerals. Attendance in 1872 was 240,920, nearly half the entire population of New South Wales. A new wing was later added to the museum facing William Street, it was nothing like Barnet's original proposal and was built to an austere modern design.

A free 30 minute orientation tour through the Museum starts on the ground floor at 10.00 a.m. 12 noon and 2.00 p.m. See the exhibition Mammals in Australia, and ponder the sad fate of those no longer in existence, including the Thylacine (Tasmanian Tiger), once the largest living marsupial carnivore, deliberately hunted to extinction in Tasmania by the mid 1930s because they killed sheep. Other Australian creatures no longer with us include the pig-footed bandicoot and the Toolache wallaby.

Lust after the gemstones in the Planet of Minerals. Experience the Dreamtime of the aboriginal culture in the Aboriginal Australia exhibit, where it's not hard to feel a twinge of sadness at the tragedy of a dispossessed people who in 200 years have abruptly woken up to the realities of modern civilisation while the rest of the Western world has had 20,000 years to get used to the idea. Aussie fossils on display include an example of the largest known bird that ever lived in the world, which became extinct about six million years ago. It was even bigger than the famed elephant bird of Madagascar, and its fossilised remains were discovered in the Northern Territory.

Victoria Barracks

Turn left at Taylor Square into Oxford Street, Victoria Barracks is twenty minutes walk up on the right. The barracks, an immaculate example of Georgian architecture and one of the best preserved colonial barracks in the world, are open to the public every Thursday at 10.00am, for an interesting free guided tour of the grounds conducted by ex-servicemen. After the tour a changing of the guard takes place accompanied by music from the 2nd Military District Band. The barracks are closed in December and January. Included in the tour is a visit to the army museum in the old military prison of the barracks, where there are displays of arms, uniforms and memorabilia from the various campaigns the Australian Army has been involved in over the years.

Victoria Barracks was constructed between 1841 and 1848 by Lieutenant Colonel George Barney of the Royal Engineers, with the help of 150 French-Canadian convicts transported to Australia following rebellions in Canada in 1837-38, and non-convict stonemasons and carpenters. Built to accommodate a British Regiment of 800 soldiers and

The main block at Victoria Barracks was for many years Australia's longest building.

The clock tower of Paddington Town Hall.

Properties at Paddington had become dilapidated by the 1940s but then it became fashionable to live in terraces close to the city centre and they were restored.

Sunset on mid-winter's day photographed from Mrs Macquarie's Point.

Previous page: Sydney Opera House floodlit for the 2000 Sydney Festival.

their families, the barracks was the base of British garrison regiments in Sydney until the first New South Wales Artillery and Infantry units were raised in 1870. Although the sandstone for the walls was quarried in Sydney, the slate on the roof of the barracks, the iron columns of the verandahs, the windows, many interior fittings and most of the cedar joinery work was brought out from England.

Paddington

Outside the barracks cross Oxford Street to Glenmore Road for a walking tour of Paddington to see the terraced houses. The whole district has been classified by the National Trust as an example of architecture worthy of preservation. Most of the terraces were built by working-class men when the area was sub-divided and sold off for building in the 1880s and 1890s. Because the lots were bought and built on by individuals rather than developers, there's a tremendous variety of style in the houses, particularly in their white facades decorated in cast iron lace-work.

Follow Glenmore Road into Gurner Street and turn right up Cascade Street, that follows the line of old Glenmore Falls, used as a source of water for a gin distillery operating in the area early last century. Pass through Paddington Street and Jersey Road to rejoin Oxford Street.

IN THE STEPS OF THE FIRST FLEETERS

From Circular Quay, follow the paved walkway around the cove to Circular Quay East. Continue north along Circular Quay East for a short distance, then ascend Moore Stairs (1868) on the right to Macquarie Street. Cross Macquarie Street to enter the park opposite and taking the centre path go through the gates (open 8.00 a.m. to sunset) outside Government House, turn left and follow the road that skirts the grounds of Government House before entering the Royal Botanic Gardens. The grassy slope just here is a good location to take photos of the Opera House. Walk down the path, through the entrance gate to the Botanic Gardens and across the forecourt to the Opera House.

Sydney Opera House

The story of the Opera House is an opera in itself. The English composer Eugene Goossens, a direct descendant of Captain Cook, was appointed Conductor of the Sydney Symphony Orchestra in 1947. Goossens persuaded the government of the day that Sydney should have its own Opera Theatre and that it should be built on Bennelong Point opposite the Harbour Bridge. In March 1956, the year following the announcement by the Government of Bennelong Point as the site for an Opera House, Goossens' luggage was searched by customs at the airport when he was returning from an overseas trip, and found to contain a quantity of pornographic photos, films and books. Goossens was tried and found guilty of importing indecent material. He resigned as conductor and left Australia that May.

An international design competition for the Opera House, commissioned by the N.S.W. Government in 1957, with a first prize of £5,000, received 233 entries and was won by the unanimous choice of the four judges, by 38 year old Danish architect Jorn Utzon. A team

Tudor style Government House was designed by London architect Edward Blore, special architect to William IV and then to Queen Victoria. The house was constructed 1837-45.

The magnificent staircase leading to the south foyers of the Opera House. Of the base or podium of the Opera House, Utzon the architect said, 'standing on the platform would be like standing on the cliffs of the Sydney Heads... the feeling under your feet... is the same as the firmness you experience when standing on a large rock'.

'It gives the impression of a wonderful piece of sculpture,' wrote Denis Winston on seeing the competition winning design in January 1957.

31

Left Page. Looking straight down on the shells. The structure of the podium was intended by Utzon 'to give the rock-like character desired for the base, as a contrast and anchor to the soaring roofs'.

Stairs leading to the upper seating and north foyer of the Concert Hall.

The north foyer of the Opera Theatre.

Flights of stairs leading from the Concert Hall foyer to the bar area have a gentle curve on them.

The interior of the Concert Hall was designed by Peter Hall, who took over as design architect at the Opera House following the resignation of Jorn Utzon.

of quantity surveyors examined the top 10 designs from the competition, and worked out that Utzon's plan would cost about $7 million to build, the cheapest they thought, of the 10 they looked at. It was decided that the Opera House would take three years to complete.

To finance the project, a public lottery 'The Opera House Lottery' was started. Tragedy struck when following the publicity surrounding the awarding of one of the first prizes of $200,000, the winner's son, eight year old Graeme Thorne, was kidnapped, held to ransom, then murdered after the ransom was paid.

Construction of the Opera House proceeded slowly, largely due to design and construction difficulties associated with the unique architecture of the project. In February 1966, with construction still proceeding on the Opera House shells, Utzon resigned following disagreements with the Country Party Minister Davis Hughes; Minister for Public Works in the new Liberal-Country Party Coalition Government. Pressured for completed working drawings of the interiors, with arguments raging over fees and the structural feasibility of the ceiling of one of the theatres, Utzon wrote in his letter of resignation '… there has been no collaboration on the most vital items of the job in the last many months from your department's side'. Talking of 'malice in Blunderland' and later saying 'I do not care if they pull the Opera House down', Utzon asked that his name should no longer be associated with the Opera House.

Utzon's design for the interior of the Opera House was shelved (the drawings were not complete), and the design of the interior and the completion of the project was overseen by a team of four Australian architects, with Peter Hall as design architect.

By the time the Opera House was officially opened by the Queen on Saturday October 10, 1973, fifteen years after construction had started, the final cost of the project had increased to $102 million. Jorn Utzon declined his invitation to attend the opening, and to date has never returned to Australia to see his completed masterpiece.

The years following the completion of the Opera House have proved its success, not only as a design exercise, but as a performance venue. The acoustics of the Concert Hall are rated very highly, while the complex of five theatres at the Opera House is one of the busiest performing arts centres in the world, with an average of over 2,900 events held every year, from conventions to grand opera.

Opera House Tours

Guided tours of the Opera House leave approximately every half an hour, seven days a

Cadman's Cottage, the oldest house in the City of Sydney. Government Coxswain John Cadman lived there with his wife Elizabeth Mortimer, who he married when he was 72 and she 33. Elizabeth was transported for stealing two brushes and some knives.

George Street.

The copper sheathed domes of Sydney Observatory still rumble round on their original bearings of cannon balls.

Victorian terraces on Argyle Place seen from Argyle Green, Sydney's only village green.

The interior of the Garrison Church. The church is one of many in Sydney designed by self-taught architect Edmund Blacket.

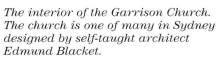

Lower Fort Street The Rocks from Observatory Hill.

week, from the lower concourse walkway on the south-west side of the Opera House. A tour fee is charged. Privately conducted tours of the Opera House are available and backstage tours on Sundays. Seats for theatres can be booked by phoning the Sydney Opera House Box Office. Alternatively, if you wish to call at the box office itself, it is in the Opera House foyer, accessible from the staircase leading up from the vehicle concourse.

From the Opera House, return to Circular Quay, walk past the ferry wharves and turn right onto Circular Quay West to reach Cadman's Cottage, near the Overseas Passenger Terminal.

The Rocks was the first area of white settlement in Australia. When the 1,030 people of the First Fleet, including 500 male, 200 female convicts and 13 children, landed in January 1788, they cleared the bush, and built a bakery, a store, a hospital, men's and women's camps and huts for the soldiers from trees, bark and branches of local mimosa or 'wattle' as they called it after 'wattle and daub'.

The building of Circular Quay itself was supervised by Colonel George Barney, designer of Victoria Barracks. In a work that took seven years, involved the labour of thousands of convicts and the quarrying of tens of thousands of tons of rock from harbour headlands, islands and Argyle Cut, Barney reclaimed five hectares at the estuary of the Tank Stream, dredged Sydney Cove using the 'Hercules' a locally built steam dredge and built sea walls to form the horse-shoe shaped 'Semi-Circular Quay'.

The cannons are all that remain from the former Dawes Point Battery.

The Rocks

Cadman's Cottage, unused and derelict in 1972, has been restored to resemble its original condition by the National Parks and Wildlife Service, who have an information centre inside. The cottage, the oldest dwelling in Sydney, was built in 1816 for John Cadman, transported to Australia in 1798 for stealing a horse. Cadman was made Government Coxswain by Macquarie, received a conditional pardon, and was later promoted to 'Superintendent of Government Boats', a post he held from 1827 to 1846, when he retired aged 88.

Walk up the steps next to Cadman's Cottage into George Street, and turn right to the Sydney Visitors Centre in the old Sailors' Home. The centre is a mine of information on Sydney and has free maps and information booklets on the city.

Continue on George Street and turn left into Playfair Street. The sandstone *Union Bond Stores* (1841), on the corner, containing a branch of the Westpac Bank with a

Sailing trips on the Harbour take place daily on the 'Bounty', a full scale replica of the original ship of 'Mutiny on the Bounty' fame.

Pavilions in Sydney's Chinese Gardens.

Sydney Monorail leaving Harbourside Station.

banking museum upstairs, was designed by Ashley Alexander, designer of Dartmoor Prison in England.

Walk the length of Playfair Street and turn right into Argyle Street. A short distance up Argyle Street you pass the entrance to the cobbled courtyard of the Argyle Stores. The cobblestones were brought out from England as ballast in the hulls of sailing ships.

One time owner of Argyle Stores, Mary Reiby, transported to Australia as a 13 year old girl, was the most influential businesswoman and merchant in Sydney during the early part of the 19th century. Among her many achievements she worked in the setting up of the Bank of N.S.W. in 1815 (now Westpac Bank). A letter Mary Reiby wrote home to her aunt on October 8, 1792, the day after she arrived on a convict transport in Sydney, is the earliest surviving letter written by an Australian convict.

As you continue west on Argyle Street, walk through Argyle Cut. The Cut was started in 1843 by convict chain gangs, working by hand to cut rock for the seawalls and the infill at Circular Quay. The stone Princes Street Bridge over the cut and the entire length of Princes Street with its houses was demolished when the Harbour Bridge approaches were built in the 1920s.

Emerge from Argyle Cut to Argyle Place, Sydney's only village green, lined by a variety of Georgian and Victorian cottages and terraces, erected between 1840 and 1880. Argyle Place was named in 1810 by Governor Macquarie after his home county in Scotland.

At the east end of Argyle Place near Argyle Cut, Holy Trinity Church known as the 'Garrison Church', was used by soldiers of Dawes Point Battery. The first military church in Australia with a foundation stone laid in 1840, it was built from stone quarried by convicts at Argyle Cut. The Garrison Church was enlarged to a design by Edmund Blacket, completed 1878.

Coming out of the church, cross Argyle Street, go up the steps on the left and follow Watson Road and Upper Fort Street to Observatory Hill. The Observatory and Astronomer's Residence stand on the site of Fort Phillip Citadel, a hexagonal redoubt with sides 100 feet long started in 1804 by Governor King to be used as a last line of defence by the Government if there was an insurrection by political prisoners. However, the fort was never used and it didn't save Governor Bligh who was overthrown by his own military in 1808. The fort was demolished in the 1840s except for two of the walls which form part of the enclosure of the Sydney Observatory.

The telescopes in the Observatory were used for astronomical research from 1858 to 1982 when the Observatory closed. The building now houses a museum. A time ball on the weather vane on the tower of the Observatory dropped daily at 1.00 p.m. as a signal for a

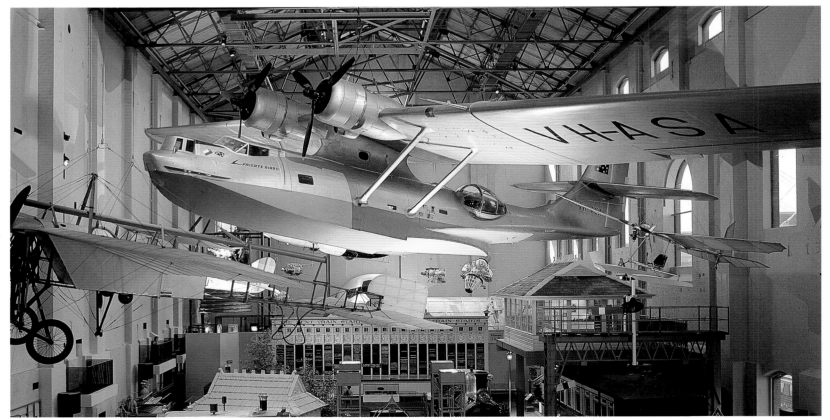

A Catalina flying boat in the space and aviation section of the Powerhouse Museum.

cannon to be fired from Dawes Point and then Fort Denison between 1858 and 1942. The practice was stopped that year following the Japanese midget submarine attack on Sydney Harbour, as it was feared the noise might alarm Sydney residents.

Firing of the gun resumed in 1986, and the dropping of the time ball (now on the sound of the gun) in 1987. Walk south from the Observatory, skirting the cutting of the Cahill Expressway, to the National Trust Centre; since 1975 the headquarters of the N.S.W. Branch of the Australian National Trust. The Trust offices are located in a building built in 1815 as a Military Hospital by Governor Macquarie, designed by his young aide-de-camp, Lieutenant John Watts. Originally constructed with double-storeyed verandahs similar to the Mint Museum, the present neo-classical facade was added by colonial architect Mortimer Lewis in 1871. Behind the main building, the S.H. Ervin Gallery of Australian Art and Architecture is housed in an old ward added to the military hospital in 1841.

Backtracking the same way you came towards the Observatory, descend Agar Steps to Kent Street, turn right and walk to Argyle Place. Enter the Lord Nelson Hotel on the corner of Kent Street and Argyle Place.

The Lord Nelson Hotel

The white sandstone Lord Nelson Hotel carries the honour of being Sydney's oldest hotel. The first landlord was an ex-convict plasterer, William Wells, who erected the building as his home in 1834 using sandstone blocks quarried from the base of Observatory Hill.

Dixon Street in Chinatown.

These days the Lord Nelson is advertised as 'The pub that restored Nelson's eyesight.' The pub brews its own beers in-house, offering a choice of Trafalgar Pale Ale, Victory Bitter, Quayle Ale or Old Admiral, 6.7% proof brewed in 'traditional dogbolter style – to be taken with great respect.' Unfortunately the Nelson's Blood Stout is no longer available. Various mementoes of the Battle of Trafalgar decorate the walls, including an original copy of the front page of the *Times* newspaper announcing the successful outcome of the battle.

Pass the Colonial House Museum at 53 Lower Fort Street (open 10.00 a.m. to 5.00 p.m. daily), walk right to the end of Lower Fort Street and onto the grass of Dawes Point Park beneath the Harbour Bridge approach. Lieutenant William Dawes of the First Fleet constructed a gun battery on the point in 1788 using six naval cannon from the *Sirius*. Dawes, a scientist, had been sent to the colony by the Astronomer Royal to observe Maskelyn's Comet, due to appear in the southern skies late in 1788. A telescope Dawes set up for astronomical observations came to more practical use when it was used to watch signals from the flag station near South Head.

Dawes Battery was enlarged to include five mortars, thirteen 42 pounders, a magazine, soldiers' quarters and a residence for the C.O.. These structures were demolished when the bridge was built, and all that remains today are five cannons cast in 1843 and 1844 resting peacefully on carriages on the grassy slope of the park overlooking the harbour and Opera House.

The Imax cinema looks like an ocean liner in dry-dock at Darling Harbour.

Continue on Hickson Road, forking left onto Circular Quay West to Campbell's Storehouse. Robert Campbell built the first private wharf in the colony and ran a prosperous merchant's business from his stores on the waterfront. Two restaurants and a wine bar have been tastefully incorporated into the fabric of the old stores.

DARLING HARBOUR

Hail a cab to Dixon Street in the centre of Sydney's Chinatown. Many of the restaurants offer a Chinese breakfast if you've missed your own. If it is a Friday, Saturday or Sunday you may be tempted to pick up a bargain at one of the stalls at Paddy's Market at the south end of Dixon Street. Outside the Market runs the Sydney Light Rail. From Haymarket Station at Paddy's you can take the train to Central Station in one direction, or to the Exhibition Centre, Convention Centre, Casino and Fish Markets in the other. Head to Little Pier Street north of the Entertainment Centre.

The Powerhouse Museum

Continue along Little Pier Street, up a ramp and follow the arrows to the Powerhouse Museum. It is Australia's largest museum, with over 25 exhibitions, and has occupied its present premises since 1988 when work was completed to convert the shell of the old Ultimo Power Station, (constructed 1899-1902) which provided power for Sydney's electric tram system. It's a great place to take the kids, with lots of hands on exhibits, and needs more than one visit to do it justice.

Sydney Aquarium and Hotel Nikko at Darling Harbour.

There is quite an extraordinary array of objects on display, relating to every branch of the applied sciences. Search out the Shorter-Slater collection of English Doulton porcelain; to say nothing of the displays of clothing, furniture, clocks, cars, planes, trains, musical instruments, collections of weapons and an exhibit tracing the development of calculations from Egyptian times to present day computers.

One of the highlights of the museum's collection is an original Boulton and Watt steam engine, the third rotative (wheel turning) steam engine ever built and the oldest known steam engine in existence. The engine was installed in Whitbread's London brewery in 1785 to replace a mill wheel drawn by 24 horses used for grinding malt. In 1787 Samuel Whitbread entertained King George III and Queen Charlotte at his brewery, proudly showing off 'this Engine which performs the work of 35 Horfes'. The engine was a reliable source of power at Whitbreads for 102 years from 1785 to 1887, when it was replaced by a more powerful steam engine. One of the original trustees of the Museum of Applied Arts and Sciences, Professor Archibald Liversidge, happened to be in London at the time, heard about the change-over and persuaded Whitbreads to donate the engine to the museum. Quite recently a decision was made to restore the engine to steam driven power, and in 1985, on its 200th birthday, it ran once more under its own steam.

The Powerhouse is open 10.00 a.m. to 5.00 p.m. daily (closed Christmas Day and Good Friday). There is a small entrance charge.

The Chinese Gardens

Opposite the museum in Darling Harbour is the Chinese Gardens. The 'Garden of Friendship' was designed according to southern Chinese tradition by Sydney's sister city, Guangzhou in China. A double-storey pavilion, 'the Gurr', stands above a surrounding system of interconnected lakes and waterfalls. Intended to 'capture the mood of a forest refuge in the bustling city' the bubbling brooks and waterfalls backed by cherry and lychee trees represent the hills and mountain springs of a landscape in southern China.

Follow the pathways around the landscaped gardens and over bridges before resting at the Tea House where the scent of lotus flowers mingles with that of freshly brewed tea and traditional cakes. The Garden is open daily from 9.30 a.m. to 6.00 p.m. There is a small entrance charge.

The former RAN destroyer 'Vampire' at the National Maritime Museum was built at Cockatoo Island in Sydney.

Sydney Exhibition Centre.

Harbourside shops on Cockle Bay, Darling Harbour.

On the opposite side of the bay Cockle Bay Wharf offers a choice of bars and restaurants.

Below: Star City Casino on Pyrmont Bay.

The interior of St Andrew's Cathedral.

The Exhibition Centre

Leaving the Gardens, walk through Tumbalong Park with its fountains and groves of native eucalypts. The Port Jackson Fig tree within the park is affectionately known as 'Fred'.

On the right near Cockle Bay a curved silver structure decorated with a chequer-board yellow and black feature is the Imax Theatre. The theatre has the world's biggest movie screen.

On the left of the park lies the Exhibition Centre which covers a massive 25,000 square metres of column-free space under the one roof. Opened in January 1988, the centre is designed to hold major international exhibitions. The glassed eastern facade is stepped back in five separate stages that can be partitioned off to form smaller halls. The fifth hall is linked by a covered walkway to the Convention Centre. Continue north along walkways lined by palm trees and pass under the flyover to Cockle Bay.

Continue your stroll alongside Cockle Bay. On your left the Harbourside Shopping Centre has 200 shops to tease your wallet and 54 assorted food outlets to tempt your palate.

The National Maritime Museum

Walk underneath Pyrmont Bridge to the National Maritime Museum, which focuses on the history of Australia's links with the sea from the earliest times to the present. Alongside the museum's two wharves you can see a number of ships including the '*Vampire*', a former RAN destroyer and '*Akarana*', a restored 1888 11.9 metre gaff cutter which was New Zealand's Bicentennial gift to Australia. One of the most historically interesting vessels on display is the *Krait*, used on operation Jaywick during the Second World War. The *Krait* was a Singapore-based Japanese fishing boat captured in the early part of the war which carried a group of Australian commandos to Singapore Harbour to plant mines on Japanese shipping. Forty thousand tons of shipping went to the bottom of the Harbour and all the commandos returned safely.

If you're in the mood to lose your shirt, or win some money to buy a new one Sydney's Star City Casino is five minutes walk from the Museum.

Pyrmont Bridge

Exit the Maritime Museum, walk up the ramp onto Pyrmont Bridge and walk over the bridge in the direction of the city. Halfway across the bridge is the control cabin for the Pyrmont Bridge swing span, which regularly opens to allow leisure craft to pass into

Sydney Town Hall and the Queen Victoria Building on George Street.

Cockle Bay. The central swing span of the bridge is one of the longest in the world and the first to use electric power, available in 1902 when Ultimo Power Station commenced generating. An ingenious device permits the Monorail beam, which runs above the bridge, to remain in place for the monorail to pass over if the swing bridge is opened for vessels up to 14 metres in height, or to swing open with the bridge for the passage of higher vessels. An automatic cut out works in the latter case to prevent the monorail carriages plunging off the end of the rail into the harbour.

Sydney Aquarium

Descend the escalator at the east end of Pyrmont Bridge and turn left for Sydney Aquarium where 50 tanks and two walk-through oceanariums have 350 species from Harbour prawns to saltwater crocodiles and the infamous Aussie shark. Open daily from 9.30 a.m. to 9.00 p.m.

Take the escalator back up to Pyrmont Bridge and walk up the steps to Darling Park Station to catch the monorail for an aerial view of Darling Harbour. Built in 1988, the Monorail runs in a 3.6 kilometre loop and has eight stations – Darling Park, Harbourside, Convention, Haymarket, Gardenside, World Square, Park Plaza (Town Hall) and City Centre. Buy a token at the station entrance. Children under four years old travel free.

TOWERS AND CATHEDRALS

Alight at Park Plaza (Town Hall). Outside the station, turn right into Pitt Street and then right again at Park Street and at George Street turn left and walk to St Andrew's Cathedral. The foundation stone of the Cathedral was laid by Governor Macquarie on August 31, 1819, but construction was axed on the recommendation of Colonial Commissioner Bigge and the project wasn't restarted until 1837. Architect Edmund Blacket redesigned the Cathedral in 'perpendicular Gothic' based on St Mary's Church in Oxford, England. The Cathedral was consecrated on St Andrew's Day, November 30, 1868. A chapel in the north west corner of the cathedral is paved with marble salvaged from St Pauls Cathedral London after it was bombed in the Second World War. Guided tours of the Cathedral depart daily at 11.00 a.m. and 1.45 p.m.

Continuing north on George Street, walk past the Italian Renaissance style Sydney Town Hall opened in 1889. Before the Opera House was completed the Town Hall's Centennial Hall, with seating for 2,000, was Sydney's main concert venue. The Centennial Hall's organ is one of the two largest original 19th century organs in the world, with 8,500 pipes.

The Queen Victoria Building

Cross Druitt Street to the Queen Victoria Building, a real cathedral of a shopping centre built in the 1890s, occupying an entire city block between York and George Streets and containing 200 shops and restaurants.

Turn right on Market Street, and pass the State Theatre, at No.49, a lavishly decorated picture palace opened in 1929. The foyer of the theatre has a staircase of solid marble, and a mosaic floor depicting St George and the Dragon locked in mortal combat.

Sydney Tower

Cross Market Street and walk across the Pitt Street Mall to Centrepoint. Go up three flights of escalators to the Podium Level, where lifts leave for the Sydney Tower Observation deck, (there is a lift charge), or one floor down the Gallery Level is the access point for lifts to the revolving restaurants (no lift charge).

There couldn't be a better view of Sydney at lunchtime than from one of the restaurants in Sydney Tower, or for something more down to earth try one of the eateries on the third level of the Skygarden, 970 feet down off 166 Pitt Street.

Descending from the tower, from the Gallery Level of Centrepoint walk through the shops and over the enclosed pedestrian bridge spanning Castlereagh Street into David Jones. Go down the escalator to the ground floor, and be prepared to mislay your credit cards, because the entire ground floor, in a most elegant grey marble setting, is devoted to the sale of everything for the well-dressed lady, with belts, stockings, handbags, jewellery, perfumes and cosmetics in abundance.

Turn right outside the Elizabeth Street entrance to David Jones and cross Market Street to the Sheraton on the Park Hotel at 161 Elizabeth Street. The hotel has a dramatic entrance foyer flanked by giant burgundy coloured marble columns. Enjoy a refreshing drink seated near the fountain in the tea lounge on the first floor conservatory looking across to Hyde Park.

Sydney Tower has the best view of Sydney short of going up in a helicopter.

The interior of St Mary's Cathedral.

A statue of Venus in the Royal Botanic Gardens.

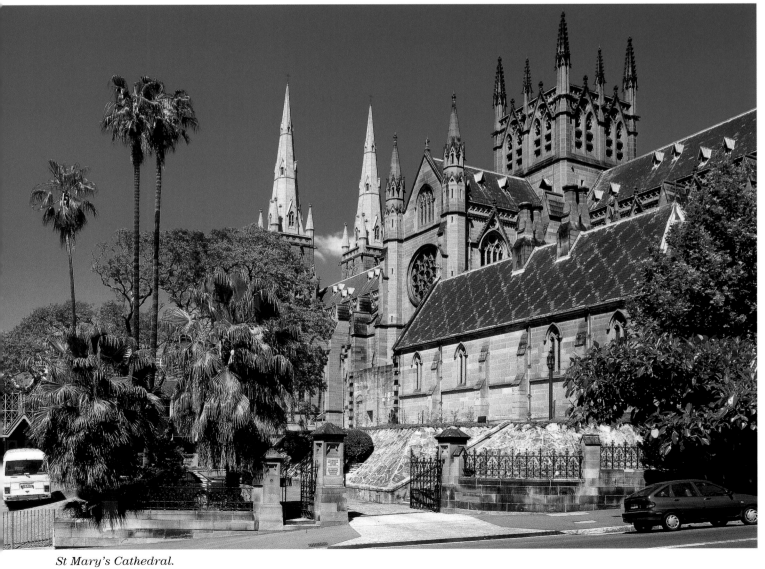

St Mary's Cathedral.

On the same side of Elizabeth Street, a little further along, is the Sydney Synagogue and museum, open to the public 12 noon to 1.00 p.m. on Tuesdays and 1.00 p.m. to 2.00 p.m. on Thursdays. Pedestrian access to the Great Synagogue is from the west side of the building around the block in Castlereagh Street.

St Mary's Cathedral

Walk up Macquarie Street and around Prince Albert Road to St Mary's Cathedral. The site of St Mary's was granted by Governor Macquarie to the first official chaplain to the colony of N.S.W., Father Joseph Therry who arrived in 1820. Macquarie laid the foundation stone of the Cathedral the following year. The original St Mary's burnt down on June 29 1865 and all that remains is part of a pillar east of the present church near the entrance to the crypt.

New designs were drawn up by architect William Wardell, construction was started in 1868 and the Cathedral was in use by 1882. Two spires topping the south facing towers that were part of the design are only now being constructed.

Doric columns flank the entry of the Art Gallery of New South Wales.

The Art Gallery

From St Mary's, walk north on College Street into Prince Albert Road past the Registrar General Department building and enter The Domain at Art Gallery Road.

Continue on Art Gallery Road past the statue of Burns to the Art Gallery of New South Wales; open daily from 10.00 a.m. to 5.00 p.m. The building housed the National Art Gallery until it moved to Canberra. Entry to the Art Gallery is free, although if a travelling world exhibition is on display there may be a charge for that section. The Gallery has permanent exhibitions on 18th to 20th century Australian Art, 17th to 20th century European Art, neo-classical sculptures and Asian Art. Among the 19th century European paintings don't miss 'The defence of Rorke's Drift 1880' by French painter, Alphonse de Neuville.

This sandstone structure in the gardens is a replica of the Choragic Monument of Lysicrates, erected in Athens about 330 BC.

A new wing of the Gallery opened in December 1988. Its four levels include a sculpture garden, contemporary collections of Australian and European prints and drawings, 20th century British and European art, an impressionist exhibition as well as a new coffee shop and theatre space.

SYDNEY ROYAL BOTANIC GARDENS

Continue on Art Gallery Road over the bridge over the Cahill Expressway and enter the Royal Botanic Gardens by the gate on the left.

The site of the gardens was the first place in Sydney to be successfully cultivated by members of the First Fleet. By July 1788 on some alluvial soil either side of a small stream that ran into Farm Cove, a Government Farm had been established with 'nine acres of corn'. One of the Tolpuddle Martyrs, Joseph Gerrald, transported in 1794, built a cottage and farmed the area. Gerrald died in 1796 and was buried east of the creek.

Mrs Macquarie's Road

In 1816 Governor Macquarie completed a road about three kilometres long that ran from Old Government House around Farm Cove to the Point and back to Government House. Macquarie's wife, Elizabeth, made daily journeys in her carriage on the road and would stop at the point to relax and admire the scenery. That same year Macquarie appointed Charles Fraser, a soldier from his 46th Regiment of Highlanders to the post of 'Superintendent of the Botanic Gardens'.

Fraser visited Norfolk Island and New Zealand, Tasmania, Western Australia and Queensland collecting plants and seeds and exchanged seeds with other botanists overseas. Fraser died in 1831. His successor, Richard Cunningham was speared to death by aborigines on the Bogan River collecting plant specimens whilst on Thomas Mitchell's expedition of 1835. Ever since, an appointment as live-in Superintendent of the Botanic Gardens has been accepted with pride and as an honour, with most Superintendents holding the post for 20 or more years. Charles Moore enjoyed a particularly long stint as superintendent for 48 years from 1848-1896.

The Gardens were renamed the Royal Botanic Gardens following the visit of Queen Elizabeth in 1954, the first reigning British Monarch to visit the country. She stepped ashore in Sydney at the Botanic Gardens on the east side of Farm Cove.

Amble through the gardens at will, to arrive at Mrs Macquarie's Point. Whichever direction you take the Gardens are delightful. The Australian native plants have the blue labels. Look out for some of the 95 species of birds that have been seen in the Gardens over the years,

Mrs Macquarie's Chair. Macquarie had the bench chiselled out so his wife Elizabeth Campbell could ride from Government House in her carriage to enjoy the view.

you have a good chance of spotting the common ones, Kookaburras, Sulphur-crested Cockatoos, White Ibis and the Blue Wren. At dusk brush-tailed possums come out and at certain times of the year flying foxes descend on the Gardens in great numbers.

Next to the creek just south of the kiosk, in the centre of the gardens, a small plaque marks the site of the first Government Farm. On the east side of Farm Cove near the Fleet Stairs, a plain sandstone wall decorated with the Royal Crest commemorates the landing of Queen Elizabeth in 1954.

At the bus stop on Mrs Macquarie's Road near the Point, the regular Sydney Explorer Bus can be picked up which will take you to Elizabeth Bay House. Alternatively, it's about half an hour's walk. If you opt for the latter, follow the path around the point, past Mrs Macquarie's Chair. After five minutes walk you will pass The Andrew (Boy) Charlton Pool on Woolloomooloo Bay. In 1924, 16 year old Andrew Charlton beat Arne Borg, the Swedish World Champion, in a race at the Domain Baths, just here. Charlton went on to win a gold and silver medal at the Paris Olympics.

A few minutes walk after passing the pool, descend a flight of concrete steps past an electric sub-station into Lincoln Crescent, turn left along Cowper Wharf Roadway passing the Bells Hotel and Woolloomooloo Bay Hotel, then as you turn into Brougham Street ascend the broad flight of McElhone Stairs directly in front.

Garden Island

Walking through the gardens on Woolloomooloo Bay and as you climb McElhone Stairs you will, no doubt, have noticed some destroyers and other ships moored at Garden Island Naval Base. As its name implies, the base was once an 11 acre island lying 200 metres off Potts Point. When the First Fleet arrived in Sydney the sailors from *HMS Sirius* cleared the vegetation on part of the island for a vegetable garden and it has been known as Garden Island ever since. On some rocks on top of the island the initials of some of the sailors have been carved with the date 1788. The calling cards of these First Fleet Kilroys are protected by three glass pyramids.

On May 31, 1942, three Japanese midget submarines entered Sydney Harbour. A torpedo fired at ships moored at Garden Island, hit the wharf next to the Kuttabul, an old ferry being used as a dormitory, blowing off the stern of the ferry and killing 19 ratings. Two of the submarines were sunk by depth charges, the third was never found. The two damaged submarines were recovered and their best halves were welded together to make a complete submarine, which takes pride of place outside the Australian War Museum in Canberra.

Between 1940 and 1944 the island was joined to the mainland by the reclamation of 14 hectares of seabed during the building of the Captain Cook Dry Dock, a considerable feat of engineering at the time. Garden Island is open on special occasions, advertised in the local press.

The Palm Grove was established in 1853 for possible oil, palm sugar or fibre industries in Australia.

A glimpse of Sydney Opera House from the Gardens.

Elizabeth Bay House on Elizabeth Bay. Most of the built-up land in the picture was once part of the grounds of the house.

Elizabeth Bay House

At the top of McElhone Stairs cross leafy Victoria Street walk to the end of Challis Avenue, cross Macleay Street, walk through the alley opposite and turn right on Onslow Avenue to reach Elizabeth Bay House.

Elizabeth Bay House, in a quiet cul-de-sac on Elizabeth Bay, with a view overlooking the harbour, is a world away from the sleaze of Kings Cross just around the corner. The unpretentious exterior gives no clue to the treasure-trove of antiques within. The domed saloon of Elizabeth Bay House and elliptical stairway are considered particularly fine examples of colonial architecture.

In October 1826, Alexander John Macleay, who had recently arrived from England to take up a post as Colonial Secretary, was granted 54 acres of land at Elizabeth Bay. Macleay employed the architect John Verge to design a 'Grecian Villa' for the site. Built between 1835 and 1838 the completed house was regarded as the finest in the colony.

The Herb Garden in the Royal Botanic Gardens.

When the house passed out of the ownership of the Macleay family early this century, the rot quickly set in. A Botanical Garden surrounding the house was engulfed by development, the kitchen wing was demolished and the house was successively a colony for artists, a venue for society weddings and dances, partitioned and turned into 15 flats and finally an unused residence for the Lord Mayor of Sydney. The rot stopped in 1977, when the Historic Houses Trust of N.S.W. acquired Elizabeth Bay House and painstakingly restored it to the period 1838-1845.

In 1845 when Alexander Macleay was in financial trouble, he sold the house to his son and the contents were sold to furnish the newly completed Government House. An inventory made of the contents at the time still exists, so it has been possible to reproduce faithfully the furnishings of the period. In 1873 William John Macleay, Alexander Macleay's son's cousin, donated the family's insect, botanical, anthropological and geological collections to Sydney University where they can be viewed today in the Macleay Museum.

Ku-ring-gai Chase National Park

The Gibberagong Waterholes Track crosses this mossy gully on the way to Bobbin Head.

Ku-ring-gai Chase National Park

A lonely cabbage tree palm near McCarr's Creek.

For the existence of Ku-ring-gai National Park we are indebted to Ecclestone du Faur, the great-grandson of a Frenchman who moved to England in 1765 who himself emigrated to Australia in 1853 aged 20. Du Faur was an independently wealthy classics scholar, educated in Greek and Latin at Harrow, yet he found a job in Sydney as a draughtsman at the New South Wales Department of Lands. Later, while chief draughtsman at the Department, du Faur bought 25 acres on Eastern Road in a district he called Turramurra after the Terramerragal clan of Guringai speaking aborigines who used to live in the area.

One of du Faur's interests was the arts, he was the driving force behind the formation of the Art Gallery of N.S.W., he also loved the Blue Mountains, where he was one of the founders of the settlement at Mount Wilson, and he had a keen interest in exploration, once financing an expedition to search for the missing explorer Ludwig Leichhardt, yet his great passion was the large area of creeks and bushland that backed onto the home he built at Turramurra. Du Faur would spend much of his spare time roaming the bush, and tried to persuade Sir Henry Copeland, the Minister for Lands, to set aside the area between Turramurra and the Hawkesbury as a National Park 'in the interests of this rapidly increasing neighbourhood' and to prevent the 'reckless destruction of native flowers' which were being ruthlessly uprooted and carried away by professional flower sellers. But the Minister wasn't having any, insisting that (Royal) National Park was already perfectly adequate for Sydney.

Du Faur now tried a little gentle diplomacy, in 1892 inviting the Governor of New South Wales the Earl of Jersey for a walk from Turramurra into the bush for a picnic then a trip by boat along Cowan Creek to promote his cause. Though all didn't go according to plan, the Governor got lost in the bush and when he was eventually located after a frantic search the tide had gone out leaving the boats at Cowan Creek high and dry on the mud and they never had their boat excursion. However, the little expedition seemed to have helped his cause, because 14,000 hectares of bushland and foreshore were set aside in 1894 as the second National Park in Australia.

Sir Henry Copeland appointed himself President of the Board of Trustees of the new reserve, which he named Ku-ring-gai in deference to the original Guringai Aborigines who occupied the area, while du Faur, who shouldered the lion's share of the work of administering the park, became managing trustee. Du Faur had an uphill battle extracting funds for the development of the park through the Department of Lands, because his requests for remuneration went to Copeland, who in his capacity as Minister for Lands, religiously wrote to himself in his capacity as President of the Park Trustees to ask for funding, who then religiously wrote back to himself as Minister for Lands regretting that no funds were currently available. As a result du Faur helped pay for some of the early development expenses himself, including the construction of the first road from Turramurra to Bobbin Head in 1901.

Since its formation the area of the park has been preserved largely intact, though some unsuccessful planners would have wished it otherwise. They included Mr Oliver Jones, who when suggestions were being made for the site of a new Commonwealth capital at the end of the nineteenth century offered a plan for a metropolis christened 'Paccivica' on the land between Cowan and Smith's creeks. A series of avenues connected buildings modelled on Windsor Castle and the Houses of Parliament at Westminster.

Ku-ring-gai Chase forms Sydney's north-eastern border. Most of the park's boundary is along the shore of the waterways of the Hawkesbury, Cowan Creek and Pittwater. The park is divided into a western and an eastern section by the drowned river valley of Cowan Creek. The two sections aren't directly connected by a road so it is practical to examine then separately.

The western section of the park is easily accessible by car as the Sydney-Newcastle Freeway and Pacific Highway run close to the western boundary. So does the main north railway line, with Mt Colah, Mt Kuring-gai, Berowra, Cowan and Brooklyn stations all within a few minutes walking distance of the park. If travelling north by car a convenient diversion to see the park can be made via Bobbin Head Road and Ku-ring-gai Chase Road

Nature seems to have its own colour sense. Peeling bark on an angophora tree.

Not only does the angophora have good colour sense the trunk has an uncanny ability to spread over rocks as if it was plasticine.

Scenery just beyond the mangrove boardwalk at Bobbin Head.

The mountain devil, so-called because the seed pod has two horns like a devil. Seen at Ku-ring-gai Wildflower Garden off Mona Vale Road.

The delicate bells of native fuschia heath, seen on the Sphinx Track to Bobbin Head.

One of the many varieties of banksia found in Ku-ring-gai Chase.

to the freeway at Mt Colah. General information on the park with routes of walking tracks is available free from the attendants at the park gates. Information is also available from the National Parks Shop at Bobbin Head and from the Visitor Centre not far past Bobbin Head on Ku-ring-gai Chase Road.

Wildlife

Though dingoes, emus and grey kangaroos no longer frequent Ku-ring-gai Chase, there are still many species of Australian fauna in the park, those recorded include 28 native mammals, 38 reptiles, 17 amphibians and more than 140 birds. Some of the more rarely seen animals include the koala, eastern pygmy possum, feather-tailed glider and the marsupial New Holland Mouse, for many years thought to be extinct then rediscovered in the park in 1967. Other animals you have a more reasonable chance of seeing include swamp wallabies, echidnas and long-nosed bandicoots.

Swamp wallabies sometimes frequent the picnic areas looking for food scraps but the best opportunity for seeing Australian animals and the magnificent Australian birdlife is to go on a bush walk, which is also the best way to see the more than 1,000 plant species in the park. It is reckoned that within the boundaries of Ku-ring-gai National Park there are more plant species than in the entire British Isles.

Walks

Among the walks in this section of the park is a nine kilometre half-day trek from Berowra Station down to Waratah Bay. The walk then meanders along the shore of Cowan Creek before climbing back up the ridge to Mount Kuring-gai Station the next stop on the line. Two other half-day walks lead to Bobbin Head from the south side of the park. The Gibberagong Track is a one-way walk leading from the end of Grosvenor Street North Wahroonga past the Gibberagong Waterholes and along the shore of Cockle Creek to Bobbin Head. Or the Sphinx Track starting near the park entrance on Bobbin Head Road follows the upper course of Cowan Creek to Bobbin Head. To make a round trip of it the Bobbin Head Track returns to the park entrance by following the ridge along the route of du Faur's original road to Bobbin Head.

The eastern section of Ku-ring-gai Chase is accessible by West Head Road off Mona Vale Road or by Pittwater Road and McCarrs Creek Road. Pittwater Road follows the shore of Pittwater to Church Point. Church Point, first known as Chapel Point, is named after a little weatherboard Methodist church which used to stand on the hillside at the point.

A pleasant way to spend the day is to take the ferry from Church Point and hop off to explore Scotland Island, Morning Bay, Lovett Bay and Elvina Bay.

Scotland Island

The ferry stops at wharves on both sides of Scotland Island, so it's possible to walk to the

Ku-ring-gai Chase Road descends through the bush from Mt Colah to Bobbin Head.

Picnic pavilions at Bobbin Head, very peaceful and quiet at late afternoon on a week-day.

Apple Tree Bay Road winds above Cowan Creek from Bobbin Head to a boat-launching ramp at Apple Tree Bay.

The start of the Gibberagong Track at Bobbin Head.

Delicate fronds on the forest floor.

Sticherus or 'umbrella ferns' growing near the Gibberagong Waterholes Track.

Deep valleys and thick rainforest vegetation provide shelter for a variety of ferns.

Detail of an umbrella fern.

A carpet of leaves on the Gibberagong Waterholes Track.

Like a tree with sunburn. Bark peeling from an angophora on the track from Berowra to Cowan Creek.

opposite side of the island, and catch a later one back. Tennis Court Wharf and Bell Wharf have public phones so you can call for a water-taxi if by chance you miss the last ferry, or alternatively you could thumb a lift from one of the locals who frequently cross to Church Point for supplies.

Morning Bay

The ferry's next stop is Hall's Wharf at Morning Bay on the west side of Pittwater. Most non-residents who alight here are going to the Youth Hostel ten minutes walk away on a track that winds uphill through the forest. The hostel is open to members of the Youth Hostels Association or to non-members at a slightly higher rate. Accommodating 32 people, the hostel is a former residence built in 1915 which was donated to the Association in 1966 by the then resident and owner Ibena Isles, a keen bush-walker.

Lovett Bay

On leaving Hall's Wharf the ferry chugs across the smooth waters of Pittwater for the short journey to Lovett Bay. When the 35,300 acres of Ku-ring-gai Chase National Park were set aside in 1894, most of the park was an inaccessible wilderness. The section of the Park along the west shore of Pittwater was easy to get to by boat, so the Park trustees set about improving access to the bush. Four men were employed at six shillings a day in April 1898 to clear the tracks to 'The Lookout', the 'Flat Rock' and the waterfall at the head of Lovett Bay. The stone signs near the ferry wharf chiselled with '1895' and 'Lovett Bay' date to this time, as does the Aboriginal face carved into the rockface behind the beach.

Elvina Bay

The final call of the ferry on the circuit before it returns to Church Point is at Elvina Bay, just 10 minutes walk away, so if you've alighted at Lovett Bay and have toured the district you can pick up the next ferry at Elvina Wharf.

McCarr's Creek Road

Pittwater Road finishes at Church Point then continues as McCarr's Creek Road into Ku-ring-gai National Park. It is one of the most picturesque stretches of road in Sydney as it winds above the yachts and waterside homes along McCarr's Creek then plunges beneath the shade of the trees in the National Park. Don't miss 'Cicada Glen', a rainforest gully just off McCarr's Creek Road on the left next to the hairpin as the road enters the National Park. It's well worth taking twenty minutes to follow the creek up into a little lost world of creepers, moss covered rocks and rainforest.

A lush gully on the Jerusalem Bay Track.

Lovett Bay, Rocky Point and Scotland Island.

Akuna Bay on Liberator General San Martin Drive.

Upper Gledhill Falls on McCarr's Creek.

Liberator General San Martin Drive hugs the shore of Coal and Candle Creek.

The drowned river valley of Cowan Creek with Lion Island in the distance.

Akuna Bay and Cottage Point

Ten minutes drive along McCarr's Creek Road from Church Point brings you to the tollbooth on West Head Road at the entry to the National Park. There's a small entry fee for cars. Five hundred metres past the toll booth Liberator General San Martin Drive on the left leads to Akuna Bay and the road to Cottage Point. Boats are available for hire at Akuna Bay and Cottage Point, and there's a café and a restaurant overlooking the water at Cottage Point. Several picturesque picnic spots with wallabies to keep you company lead off General San Martin Drive.

West Head Road

West Head Road meanders and undulates through the bush to the spectacular lookout of West Head. There are a dozen or so tracks that lead off the road into the bush, and it is worth describing some of the more interesting ones. One of the best, which is the first on the right, is the Engravings Walking Track. As its name suggests, the track leads past some Aboriginal carvings to Elvina Bay. It then follows the old 1895 walking trail to the waterfall beyond Lovett Bay. Backtracking the same way opposite a Swiss style chalet, the Flat Rock Track heads steeply up the hill past Frederick Oliver's grave to the lookout at Flat Rock. The track then winds round to rejoin the Elvina Track to take you back to the car.

The Basin

Another few kilometres along West Head Road on the right, a track leads to The Basin and there's a branch off it leading to Currawong and Great Mackerel Beach. The beaches are also accessible by the ferry which leaves from Snapperman Beach at Palm Beach.

The Basin really is a beautiful spot, 50 acres of lawn dotted with trees and a line of Norfolk Island pines along the shore backed by wooded hills that rise to a height of 150 metres. One imagines that if it had been on the Mediterranean the Greeks would have built a temple there. The Basin has a sandy beach with a view across Pittwater to Palm Beach and Barrenjoey headland, and at the 'Inner Basin' a large saltwater lagoon washed clean by the tides is made safe for swimming by a shark net stretched across the entrance. It's not a half-bad place to while away a Sunday, or if you wish to linger longer you can take a tent and provisions on the ferry and book a campsite at a very reasonable rate through the National Parks and Wildlife Service. There are shower blocks, a toilet and freshwater supply available.

Currawong Beach

Next stop on the ferry after The Basin is Currawong Beach – it used to be known as Little Mackerel Beach but was re-named in 1977. In 1910 the beach and 48 acres on the flat were bought by Dr Bernard Stiles of Newtown and his wife, and they built a cottage called 'Midholme' there. Since 1950 Midholme and nine other cottages have been owned by the Labour Council of New South Wales. The cottages are available through the Labour Council for lettings, with slightly cheaper rates for union members. For your entertainment besides the beach, and walks along the creek, there's a tennis court and a nine-hole golf course.

Mackerel Beach

Last stop on the ferry before it heads back to Palm Beach is Great Mackerel Beach. The

Grass trees on the heights above Refuge Bay. Aborigines used to make spears from the seed stems.

The sheltered waters of The Basin.

Currawong Beach.

A ferry has just left the wharf at Mackerel Beach for Palm Beach.

Refuge Bay.

beach is also accessible by a steep track that climbs up and over the headland from Currawong Beach. Promoted by the real estate company selling blocks there in 1920 as 'The Balmoral of Pittwater', a brochure described to prospective buyers

> the … picturesque lagoon … encompassed on the land side, by a buttress of noble hills, on the lower slopes of which a chain of knolls (every one an ideal site for a bungalow) leads sheer into fairyland … The gully … is overhung with palms and tree ferns and the usual tangle of semi-tropical foliage … Thence, amidst alternate sunshine and shadow tracks radiate in all directions through scenes of sylvan loveliness to innumerable points of interest.

These days Great Mackerel Beach is a village of 100 or so houses with streets of grass instead of bitumen between the homes, which sell for Balmoral type prices if they ever come up for sale.

West Head Lookout

Another six kilometres relaxing drive from The Basin Track brings you to the car park at West Head lookout on Commodore Heights. The Heights, which rise to nearly 200 metres, were named after Commodore Lambert, Captain of the Royal Navy ship *H.M.S. Challenger* which was in Australian waters between 1866 and 1870. A short walk brings you to a lookout on the headland with a quite superb view of Pittwater, Palm Beach and Broken Bay. If you tire of the views you can feed your chicken sandwich to the tame kookaburras. There's also a giant goanna who may give you a fright as he slithers across the crazy paving keeping an eye on his territory. He's never done anyone any harm though.

Six hundred and forty acres at West Head were granted to William Lawson in 1834 as a reward for the part he played blazing the first trail across the Blue Mountains in 1813. When Ku-ring-gai National Park was proclaimed in 1894, this land was still in private ownership. It was offered to the Park trustees for £1 an acre in 1911, but was turned down. In 1929 a public road was opened out to West Head and the landowners proposed transforming the 640 acres into the 'Riviera Estate', producing a coloured brochure illustrating a country club, hotel, casino, recreation reserves and a golf course. The remainder of the land was to be sold for 2,500 house lots. However the scheme never got off the ground during the Depression.

In 1940 50 acres were resumed at West Head and the headland transformed into 'West Fortress', with gun emplacements close to the waterline linked by a tram-line, observation posts, search light positions, an anti-submarine boom across Barrenjoey Head and a military camp on the heights.

Resolute Beach

From West Head a track leads south down to two secluded beaches on the shore of Pittwater. A climb back up the hill and a left turn at the track junction above the beach leads after a further 20 minutes walk to Resolute Beach, no doubt named after the schooner *Resolute*, which on 1st May 1877 according to the following day's *Sydney Morning Herald*, bound 'for Sydney from the Richmond, parted her chains this morning, and went ashore under West Head. She is bilged and full of water. The crew are safe'.

There are no roads, just grass between the houses at Mackerel Beach.

Palm Beach from West Head Lookout.

Sydney's Northern Beaches

An aerial view of Manly and the Northern Beaches from Manly Cove.

Sydney's Northern Beaches

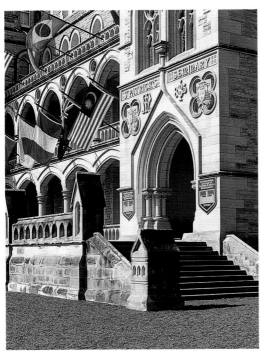

Beautiful stonework on St Patrick's Seminary.

Manly has a timeless quality about it. Somehow one imagines the Corso, the pines and the promenades have always been there, but they are relatively new. Indeed Manly was virtually uninhabited for the first 60 years of white settlement even though Governor Phillip discovered and graced the peninsular with a name before discovering and naming Sydney.

In January 1788 Phillip set out to explore Sydney Harbour from Botany Bay and spent the first night at Camp Cove. Later the following day, as he related in a despatch to Lord Sydney:

> The boats, in passing near a point of land in the harbour, were seen by a number of men, and twenty of them waded into the water unarmed, received what was offered them, and examined the boats with a curiosity that gave me a much higher opinion of them… and their confidence and manly behaviour made me give the name of Manly Cove to this place.

Manly continued as a camping ground for a local aboriginal tribe until 1810, when Macquarie, on his first day as Governor, granted the first land rights. However, for many years Manly remained bush and sandhills. In 1822 there were only two families resident there and by 1841, according to the official census, there were 25 people living in four houses in Manly. It wasn't until 1853, when Henry Gilbert Smith 'The father of Manly' took an interest in the district that everything changed. Smith thought Manly was like a dream come true, later describing it to a friend:

> It's situation – seven or eight miles by water from Sydney, is as fine a thing as you can imagine and it takes in the only ground which has the sea beach on one side and a fine sandy cove on the other. There is no place to equal it for beauty. It is truly delightful. There is nothing like it in the wide, wide world…

'Gentleman Smith' as he was known by the locals, was a native of Northamptonshire, England, who emigrated to Australia and became a successful merchant and land speculator. In May 1853 Smith bought 20 acres of land in Manly for £8 an acre including some rising ground on the hill west of the Harbour Beach which he called 'Fairlight' after a village near Hastings. The following year Smith built 'Fairlight House' on the hill, a handsome stone residence with wide verandahs and a view across Sydney Harbour to the Heads, and completed a 50 foot jetty on Manly Cove as a berth for a 23 ton wooden paddle steamer *The Brothers*, Manly's first ferry.

Smith bought up more land in Manly (his holdings eventually amounted to 120 acres) and boldly set about turning the peninsular into a Brighton of the antipodes. Opposite the ferry wharf Smith built the Italienate Pier Hotel, cut a track through the bush to the Ocean Beach he called 'The Corso' after a street in Rome, and by the addition of a public 'pleasure garden', fun fair, refreshment tents and a maze had turned Manly into a resort 60 years before Bondi became popular.

To ensure the settlement's future prosperity Smith built 'a little rustic church', providing £50 a year for the salary of the clergyman, and donated the land for two other churches, a schoolhouse (which opened in 1858 with 19 pupils), a police station and a 'School of Arts'. Most of Manly's present day parks and waterside reserves were left to the people of Manly in Smith's will, including North Steyne, East and West Esplanade, Kangaroo Park and Ivanhoe Park.

The Manly ferries

Manly was effectively an island cut off from Sydney because the only way to get there except for undertaking the arduous land journey was by ferry. The ferries were the key to Manly's success and it was the creation of the ferry service that brought Smith's dream of turning Manly into a resort a reality. The *Empire* newspaper of 25th May 1859 reported that 'between 12,000 and 13,000 persons visited the beautiful indentation on Sydney Harbour known as Manly Beach' and they all travelled by ferry.

But although a significant portion of Sydney's population came to visit Manly on holidays, it wasn't a place where they immediately flocked to live. In 1856 the population was still only 73, and it wasn't until 1871 that it rose to 500. But it was that first glimpse

About the only way to get to Store Beach on Spring Cove is by boat.

St Patrick's bathed in late afternoon sunshine.

Shelly Beach is a ten minute walk along the water-front from Manly.

Norfolk Island pines on Manly promenade.

of Manly's charms after a trip on the ferry, arriving at the Harbour Beach, then strolling through The Corso to the Ocean Beach, that convinced visitors that here was a place where they should permanently reside. In 1888 the population from Manly to Narrabeen Lagoon reached 2,000, to the distress of some longer term residents. In the 1890s when two rival ferry companies were vying for business and the fare came down to 3d return (in 1854 it was a shilling each way) enormous numbers of day-trippers started to flock to the Village. This was in spite of the fact that visitors weren't allowed to swim and if they wanted to cool off had to be content with a paddle. An 1838 Act of Parliament forbade all public swimming except between the hours of 8 p.m. and 6 a.m. a situation which prevailed until 1903. It was then that the Sly Brothers started Australia's first Life Saving Service operating from an old fishing shed and with segregated swimming – males at one part of the beach, females at another. However, a wave of common sense swept the whole local surfbathing fraternity after two women drowned and the bathers were united.

In 1922 the population of Manly reached 17,000. At that time three fifths of householders at Manly had been there originally for a holiday and then decided to come back to live. The 1930's were the bleak years of the depression, but they were Manly's heyday, for everyone could still afford a few pence for the ferry fare and the tremendous crowds that flocked to Manly's beaches were double what they ever are today. The record was set on 27th January 1936 when over 100,000 passengers travelled to Manly by ferry.

A trip by ferry for the first time is a great thrill, and even for those who live in Manly and commute by ferry every day to Sydney the journey still holds a special place in their hearts.

The Corso

On arrival by ferry in Manly on a busy Sunday, you're swept along with a tide of humanity which carries you across the road and along The Corso to the Ocean Beach. The writer D.H. Lawrence came this way in May 1922 and stopped with his wife for a cup of tea. He thought Manly was 'Like a bit of Margate with seaside shops and restaurants, till you come out on a promenade at the end; and there is the wide Pacific rolling in on the yellow sand…' One of the first things you pass on The Corso on the way to the beach is Manly War Memorial, unveiled during the Great War in October 1916. The memorial was given to the citizens of Manly by Mark Mitchell, whose son was the first soldier from Manly to fall in the conflict.

Manly's pines

Entering onto the promenade next to the Ocean Beach, you are greeted by the sight of Manly's Norfolk Island pines. The pines are as much a part of Manly as the Opera House

Manly residents who work in the city can unwind on the way home with a trip on the Manly Ferry.

Surf carnival at Manly Beach.

is a part of Sydney. They are not native to Manly, the first ones were planted by Henry Gilbert Smith at Fairlight House and on the Harbour foreshore nearby. In 1877 the first Mayor of Manly, Thomas Rowe, instituted a Tree Planting Beautification Scheme for Manly. Rowe, a prospector, architect, Commander of the Engineers in the army, and father of 16 children, found time among his other duties of taking the fledgeling Municipality under his wing. He planted Moreton Bay figs in strategic locations and started plantings of Norfolk Island pines on the reserves next to the Harbour and Ocean Beaches. The young trees were brought from Norfolk Island 50 or 100 at a time then fertilised by seaweed gathered on the beach and dug into the sand. Early plantings were not very successful and a base of soil and leaf mould was found to give the seedlings a better chance. Rowe's work was carried on by subsequent mayors, and by the late nineteenth century pines were planted in a double crescent along the entire length of the Harbour and Ocean Beaches.

During the war the defence command issued an order to cut down all the pines on the Ocean Beach to provide a clear field of fire for defending artillery in case of invasion. Preparations were put in place and one pine was cut down at South Steyne near the surf club before common sense prevailed and the order was lifted. A plaque on the stump was a reminder to passers by of how Manly nearly lost its pines.

A recent and more devastating threat to the pines has been the presence in the sea water of detergents from household waste entering the ocean. Onshore winds deposit small quantities of detergent on the pine needles of the trees, stripping off their natural

Looking north on Manly Beach towards Queenscliff.

Manly Corso.

The original site for Manly Quarantine Station was chosen because it was just inside Sydney Heads at the entrance to the Harbour.

protective oils and killing them. This was particularly the case at the north end of the Beach where the trees all but disappeared. A vigorous replanting scheme has since been instituted, and household waste is now pumped further out to sea, so it shouldn't be too long before Manly's pines regain their former glory.

Shelly Beach

From the Manly Surf Club at the south end of the beach a ten minute walk leads to Shelly Beach. The path passes a café on the corner of Bower Lane. This spot is known as Fairy Bower. In the mid-nineteenth century when, the area was still a tranquil setting of flowers and ferns like a 'fairyland', it was a popular place for picnics and church outings from Manly.

Shelly Beach, comprised of millions of finely ground sea shells, is one of only two west facing beaches on the east coast of Australia. From the north end of the beach a track leads around the headland to a high lookout with a bird's eye view of Shelly Beach and Manly.

North Head

South from Manly town centre, North Head Scenic Drive continues for two kilometres through bushland to a car park on the headland. On the way the road passes beneath a sandstone archway. This is the original entrance to Manly Quarantine Station. When the Station was in use the way was barred by locked gates and a guard checked vehicles entering and leaving

At North Head a circular walking track about a kilometre long leads to a series of lookouts on the south side of the Head with views across the mouth of the Harbour to South Head and straight down the Harbour to the city. North Head is the highest and the most spectacular lookout of all the reserves on the Harbour foreshores, and provides a good vantage point for viewing the entry to Sydney of the world's great ocean liners and naval ships.

Manly Quarantine Station

On the way back to Manly is Manly Quarantine Station. Daytime tours or a night time 'ghost tour' can be arranged through the New South Wales National Parks and Wildlife Service. About 60 buildings remain at the Quarantine Station out of the 90 or so that used to occupy the site, most of them dating from the 1870s to the 1920s when the Station saw its heaviest use.

The Station was first set aside as a quarantine area in 1828, when the *Bussorah Merchant* arrived in Sydney carrying smallpox. The time taken on the journey by sea to Sydney was longer than the incubation period of all known infectious diseases, including

There's a hint of the Italian Riviera in some of Manly's early architecture.

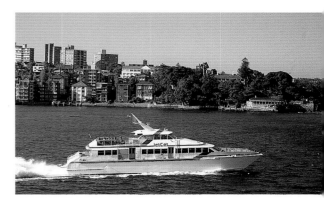

Manly Jetcat, for those without time to unwind on the ferry.

Freshwater Beach is the next one to the north of Manly.

Dawn at Dee Why Head.

Sunrise at Freshwater Beach.

Flowers in a garden on Carrington Parade near Curl Curl Beach.

Right page: Curl Curl Beach.

typhus, scarlet fever, smallpox and influenza. If a ship carried disease it broke out on board, so judicious quarantine procedures by the authorities prevented epidemics carrying to the Australian mainland. Facilities were expanded to keep pace with the passenger carrying capacity of ocean liners, so that by 1915 the Station could comfortably accommodate over 1,500 souls.

Shipping companies bringing a vessel to Sydney carrying disease were deemed responsible for any quarantine costs incurred on arrival in port, and not only paid the expenses of the station, but housed passengers in a similar style to that they'd enjoyed on board ship, waited on by the ship's crew who also cooked their meals and washed their clothes in a giant brass washing machine powered by a steam engine. Areas of the station were separated into First, Second, Third and 'Asiatic' class accommodation, each with its own restaurants, lounges and sleeping quarters. Passengers fortunate enough not to be carrying disease themselves made the most of their enforced detention, playing cricket or tennis, swimming on Store Beach, or wandering the bushland of North Head.

The Station was only in occasional use after the 1930s. During the Second World War British evacuee children were temporarily housed there on arrival and the Station was used as a billet for soldiers. The Station's final call to fame was in 1974 when 750 residents from Darwin were temporarily housed there after Cyclone Tracy devastated the town on Christmas Day. Ten years later in 1984, the Station was closed completely for quarantine purposes, and assumed its present status as a historic site.

Collins Beach and Store Beach

Leaving the Quarantine Station, continue north to Collins Beach, named after Captain David Collins, Judge Advocate with the First Fleet. It's a lovely quiet beach surrounded by natural bushland and the scene is no doubt little different today to the appearance of the Beach on 7th September 1790 when Phillip met the Aborigine, Bennelong here after receiving from him a gift of meat from a dead whale. Bennelong was an Aborigine Phillip had captured earlier at Manly, and brought back to Sydney to live with him at Government House. He had recently escaped and made his way back to Manly. On meeting Bennelong Phillip offered him a glass of wine and they were proceeding in this friendly manner when:

> ... a native, with a spear in his hand, came forward ... The nearer the Governor approached, the greater became the terror and agitation of the Indian. To remove the fear, Governor Phillip threw down a (dagger) which he wore at his side. The other, alarmed at the rattle of the (dagger) and probably misconstruing the action, instantly fixed his lance on his throwing stick ... the Indian, stepping back with one foot, aimed the lance with such force and dexterity, that striking the Governor's right shoulder just above the collar-bone, the point glancing downward came out at the back, having made a wound of many inches long.

South Curl Curl rock pool. I never tire of this view even though I drive past most mornings on my way to work.

The party quickly returned to Government House by boat, where

> …surgeons were sent for. Mr Balmain, who was the first that arrived, after examining the wound, made everybody happy by assuring them he did not apprehend any fatal consequences from it. He extracted the point of the spear and dressed the wound, and in six weeks the Governor was perfectly recovered.

Phillip insisted his men were not to take any retaliatory action against the offending Aborigine. From the south end of Collins Beach it's a ten minute clamber over the rocks at low tide to Store Beach, named after the stores left there for the early inmates of the Quarantine Station

St Patrick's

North Curl Curl rock pool. Always worth a visit when there's a big surf running.

Continuing our journey back towards Manly we pass the ornate wrought iron gates of St Patrick's seminary. During the nineteenth century over a period of eight years the Catholic church made requests to the Government for a grant of land on which to build a seminary. Requests for land at Camperdown, Coogee and Cabarita were made and refused, until finally, in 1863 Governor Bourke agreed to an application for a site in Manly. Many thought the 53 acres offered were granted out of spite, on land which the Governor thought no one would ever need, next to the unsanitary Quarantine Station and the only means of communication with Sydney by boat. In fact the church had received one of the superlative sites in Sydney, on the hill high above Manly with a view along the Northern Beaches, and in 1885 they commenced construction of a college modelled on Maynooth, the national seminary of Ireland.

Ever since it opened in January 1889 the college, perched on the hill above Manly like a medieval castle, has been one of the grandest examples of architecture in Sydney. Today the college houses the International College of Tourism and Hotel Management.

The walk to The Spit

Manly Wharf is the starting point for one of the best harbourside walks in Sydney, following the shoreline for nine kilometres to The Spit Bridge. The well maintained walkway meanders its way past Forty Baskets Beach and Reef Beach to a lookout on Dobroyd Head, then past Grotto Point and the small sandy cove of Castle Rock Beach to Clontarf. The City of Dublin in Ireland was known in ancient times as Clontarf, and was the scene of a battle in 1039 when the Irish expelled the Danes from Ireland.

On the 12th March 1868 the 23 year old son of Queen Victoria, Prince Alfred the Duke of Edinburgh was the guest of honour at a formal picnic at Clontarf while visiting Australia during a world tour. Suddenly, he was approached by Henry O'Farrell, an Irish supporter of the anti-royalist Fennian society, who produced a pistol and shot him in the back. As

Long Reef at sunrise from Dee Why Lagoon.

luck would have it the force of the bullet was partly absorbed by the Prince's india-rubber braces, and he made a full recovery after being operated on a few days later at Government House. In thanksgiving to the work of the doctors and nurses who saved his life, Alfred established a fund to build a hospital to be known as the Royal Prince Alfred.

From Clontarf the walk continues around Sandy Bay to the Spit Bridge.

The Spit is named after the sand spit that extends from the south shore of Middle Harbour. For 38 years from 1850 to 1888 Peter Ellery ran a hand punt service across the narrow channel of Middle Harbour from The Spit to the north shore. After Ellery retired a government steam punt provided a service on the crossing until 1924 when the first toll bridge opened. In its last year of operation the punt carried 300,000 motor vehicles, 20,000 cycles and 50,000 horse drawn vehicles. The toll to cross the first Spit Bridge levied from its opening in 1924 until it was lifted in 1930 more than paid for the cost of the bridge and left a profit of over £5000 used by Manly Council to widen the roadway on their side of the bridge. The present Spit Bridge with its single lift span was opened in 1958. It lifts eight times a day during the week and thirteen times a day at weekends to allow passage for yachts and ferries through Middle Harbour.

Surf carnival at Dee Why.

Manly Reservoir

A tour of Manly wouldn't be complete without a visit to Manly Reservoir. Several walks meander through the surrounding bush, swimming, boating and water-skiing are permitted on the lake and there are plenty of shady barbecue sites lining the west shore.

The lake dates to 1892 when work was completed of building a dam and pumping station across Curl Curl Creek to provide what was then expected to be a permanent freshwater supply for Manly village. When Manly Dam ceased to be used as a water supply, the lake and surroundings were turned into a War Memorial Park in memory of those who had fallen in the First World War and other conflicts.

Freshwater Beach

Heading north from Manly we reach Freshwater Beach. From the early 1900s Freshwater was a popular destination as a working man's camp. On the flat ground inland from the beach men stayed first in tents, then in purpose-built weatherboard huts with galvanised iron roofs and basic furnishings. The huts went by names such as 'The Ritz' and 'Shark Bait'. Accommodation was for men only with lady visitors allowed only on Sundays. After the First World War new lodges or 'Camps' as they were still called opened catering mainly for working class families from Sydney. Many liked Freshwater so much they later returned to live.

Dee Why. Take away the surf boats and you'd have a nomads camp on the steppes of Mongolia.

Dee Why Lagoon. A beautiful stretch of water which turns into ugly mudflats when the sand dam at the mouth is breached during heavy rains.

Seagulls at Dee Why rock pool.

'The Kiosk', the oldest building in Harbord, built in 1908 overlooking the beach, dates to the era of the camps. It was built by Mr Lewers who owned and operated one of the camps and besides providing accommodation for visitors, it was the venue for afternoon tea parties, meetings and dances. When Harbord's first Post Office was established in 1909 it opened in the Kiosk.

To lift the status of the suburb above that of a campsite, the Shire Clerk of Warringah wrote to the Post Master General's Department in 1923 regarding having

> the name of Freshwater changed to Harbord. Freshwater … has long fallen into disrepute on account of the people of doubtful and riotous character, who frequent the place at weekends in the summertime.

So Harbord became the official name of the suburb and the beach, though the beach was officially given back its title of Freshwater in 1980. The last of the camp lodges were sold in the 1930s and the sites sub-divided for housing. Freshwater Beach remained private property for nearly 100 years from the time of the original grant in 1818 until it was resumed by the Government in 1910 for 'public recreation'.

Freshwater's greatest claim to fame was in 1914, when Duke Kahanamoku asked a Sydney company to fashion a surfboard like the one he used in his native Hawaii, and gave the first demonstration of surf-board riding ever seen in Australia. In memory of this epic event there's a bronze statue of the Duke on a surfboard on the headland. His board was put on display in the Freshwater Surf Life Saving Clubhouse. When the Duke called at the Freshwater Club when he was in Australia for the 1956 Melbourne Olympics he took the board off the wall and rode the breakers at the beach once again.

During the war concrete tank traps were laid in a line west of the beach and barbed wire was strung in a maze formation across the sand. Swimmers could still use the beach, they just had to negotiate a way through the maze first!

Curl Curl Beach

Continuing around from Freshwater, we reach Curl Curl Beach (Curl Curl incidentally, is Aboriginal for lagoon). Francis Myers came this way in the 1870's, taking the coast route from Freshwater and

> swinging around by Curl Curl it opens up a great stretch of good and beautiful country, whose producing power is well shown by the garden at the head of the lagoon, which sends daily great crates of all garden produce to the village (Manly) and the city, everything useful and beautiful, from roses to cabbages.

This area around the lagoon which was such rich farmland in Myer's time is now lush green parks and playing fields.

Dee Why

A track from North Curl Curl Beach leads across the top of the cliffs for a half-hour walk

Soft rocks on Long Reef headland have been weathered into a broad rock shelf which is covered by the waves at high tide.

Dee Why Beach and Lagoon. The day won't be far away when the lagoon is completely silted up.

Collaroy rock pool.

Like pagan priests making a dawn sacrifice. Fishermen on Collaroy storm-water drain.

to Dee Why. The first known reference to Dee Why is a note written in pencil in Surveyor Meehan's field book 'Wednesday 27ᵗʰ Sept, 1815 Dy Beach – marked a Honey Suckle Tree near the beach'. A later survey by Meehan included the note 'Long Reef, Dy Lagoon'. Meehan was an Irish rebel transported to New South Wales for his part in the Dublin Uprising of 1798. Arriving in Sydney in 1800 and having had some training as a surveyor, he was immediately appointed an assistant to the Colonial Surveyor, a capacity he worked in energetically until his death in 1826. But why were the letters Dy in his notebook? The question has certainly vexed historians ever since. Was it an abbreviation of the Greek dysprosium 'hard to reach' as no doubt Dee Why then was? Was it because the shape of the lagoon resembles the letters D and Y or that the letters were carved on a rock by a sailor from the Spanish ship Dona Ysabel? I'll guess we'll never know.

But we do know that the history of Dee Why is closely tied with that of the Jenkins Family. James Jenkins arrived in Sydney as a convict in 1802 and started to buy up land holdings in the Collaroy area in the 1820s. In order to take his cattle and produce to market in Sydney, Jenkins built a road with 13 bridges from Collaroy to the water's edge at North Harbour. When he died he left his estate to his wife and eight children. By now the Jenkins' estate stretched in an unbroken line from Dee Why to Mona Vale. Elizabeth, his remaining daughter, never married and seemed content to devote her life to religion and the Salvation Army cause. Following the crash of the banks in Sydney in the 1890's Elizabeth feared she may be exposed to debts she couldn't pay and asked the Salvation Army to accept liability in return for the transfer of most of the property.

The first task undertaken by the Salvation Army on its enormous estate was to build the 'Home of Rest', a recuperation centre for Salvation Army officers. The building still stands today and is the oldest in Dee Why. The Salvation Army expanded its activities in Dee Why to include an Industrial Farm, a Sanatorium for Men to care for 'inebriates' and a Home for Little Girls. But Warringah Council was airing concerns about the large landholdings in the district for the exclusive use of the Salvation Army, including Dee Why Beach, part of the original Jenkins' estate, which the Salvation Army had fenced off as private property. In 1911 there were only five private dwellings in Dee Why. When a similar case had arisen at Harbord, where the beach was part of the holding of a previous land grant, the Government simply resumed the beach and that was that, but the Salvation Army were prepared to fight the Government in the courts to retain ownership of Dee Why Beach. However, the Government won the case and the beach was opened to the public. Within two years the Salvation Army started to sell off land for housing. The land was surveyed and subdivided for the first land sales in the period 1911-14. This was the establishment of the town of Dee Why. Once the beach was opened to the public in 1912 Dee Why Surf Life Saving Club was founded and a Surf Club was opened.

Long Reef

From Dee Why continue north towards Long Reef. Dee Why Beach and Long Reef Beach are in fact one long beach cut in two by Dee Why Lagoon. The Lagoon is a wildlife and bird refuge and although there are still birds there today it has nothing like its original numbers. The black swan is the symbol of Dee Why but is seldom seen today. In 1963 they took off en masse and left for regions unknown never to return.

Collaroy and Narrabeen

Leaving Long Reef, head north via Pittwater Road to Collaroy. On the way you pass the Salvation Army Conference Centre and Home for the Aged, built on land that was part of the original Jenkins' gift to the Salvation Army. Junius, took this way in 1861, heading to Pittwater on horseback. Writing in the *Sydney Morning Herald* in 1861 he told how:

> Passing Jenkins' farm there is a level piece of beautiful turf nearly two miles long and a quarter of a mile broad, quite fitted for a racecourse; forming, the finest gallop anywhere near Sydney.

Pittwater Road follows the line of the level turf through Collaroy and Narrabeen. Almost all the settlements on the Northern Beaches are set back from the beach with a reserve between the breakers and the first houses. Somehow at Collaroy, through the ministrations of a developer or because of a lack of civic foresight, the houses end at the sand of the beach. And at a price. In 1945 an enormous storm swept the beach and eight houses were destroyed, one of them actually floating out to sea.

The crescent of sand stretching north from Collaroy is, at nearly four kilometres, the longest of the Northern Beaches, but it is in fact two beaches, in name at least, Collaroy at the south end and Narrabeen at the north. The beach was always known as Narrabeen and Collaroy didn't exist until a coastal paddle steamer of that name lodged in the sand. In January 1882 the *Collaroy*, named after an Aboriginal word for 'long swamp reeds', was sailing south off the coast during a storm. The wind and waves drove the ship close in to the shore at Long Reef, and the Captain, seeing he wasn't going to make it round the rocks, ran the ship aground onto the beach. The ship remained stuck fast in the sand for over two and a half years, until 1884 when a new owner who had a soap and candle factory in Sydney, liberally greased her hull with soap and wax and finally wrenched it from the sand. The name Collaroy stuck as fast to the south end of the beach as the ship had stuck in the sand.

At North Narrabeen Beach a sturdy flight of wooden steps leads to the top of Narrabeen Head, a good vantage point for the view along the length of Narrabeen Beach and Narrabeen Lakes. When George Caley the botanist passed this way in 1805 he called the lake 'Cabbage Tree Lagoon'. Then in 1815 when Surveyor Meehan mapped the south shore of the lake he called it 'Narrabang Lagoon'. Meehan stated the name was Aboriginal for 'swan'. However Narrabeen was the name that came into general use. As you drive through on Pittwater Road there's a sturdy wooden bus shelter. This is the old tram shelter where D.H. Lawrence alighted on his journey to the Northern Beaches in 1922. Lawrence had caught the tram from Manly and thought Narrabeen was 'the end of everywhere, with new "stores" – that is flyblown shops with corrugated iron roofs – and with a tram shelter and little house agents booths plastered with signs'. The tramline had been extended from Brookvale to the terminus at Narrabeen as a single line track in 1913. But the service lost money nearly every year of operation before finally closing in 1939.

Cascades on Oxford Creek at Oxford Falls.

Turimetta Beach

Just north of Narrabeen is Turimetta Beach. Turimetta is one of the smallest and least known but most picturesque of the Northern Beaches, tucked away out of view of the main road. There is no suburb of Turimetta, so if you talk about Turimetta there are even many Northern Beaches residents who will look at you blankly. Steps lead down to Turimetta Beach, and at low tide you can walk over the rocks below Narrabeen Head to North Narrabeen.

Collaroy Beach and Surf Club.

Pelicans at Narrabeen Lakes getting ready for the day.

Sunrise at North Narrabeen.

Narrabeen.

A track above Turimetta Beach leads through the heath land of Turimetta Head to a lookout. It's well worth the extra effort because the lookout is even more spectacular than that on Narrabeen Head. Not only are there views south all the way to Manly but also north to Mona Vale and the headlands towards Palm Beach. North Narrabeen and Turimetta Head used to be known as Sheep Station Hill. The grassy slope was used for sheep grazing when the land was part of the original Jenkins' estate. When the property passed to the Salvation Army and it was sub-divided for housing some of the streets were named after Salvation Army officers, including Arnott Crescent and Carpenter Crescent. Arthur Arnott was a son of the Arnotts, founders of the biscuit bakers, and became a Salvation Army Captain. The firm honoured their Salvationist member by calling two of their products after him: Thin Captain and SAO biscuits, the latter standing for the Salvation Army motto 'Serve and Obey'.

Narrabeen Lakes.

Warriewood to Bungan

From Turimetta Head the track leads down the hill to Warriewood Beach. The area behind Warriewood and Mona Vale on the west side of Pittwater Road was once known as 'Crystal Valley' after the thousands of glasshouses that supplied the Sydney markets with fresh vegetables and cut flowers. The glasshouses and neighbouring market gardens were established by European migrants arriving after the First World War, many of them from Italy and Yugoslavia. During the Second World War the glasshouses were surrounded by barbed wire and trenches and bren-gun carriers were sited in strategic positions. The intention was to make them resemble factories in the hope that if there were Japanese air raids the glasshouses would be bombed instead of factories closer to Sydney. Farming remained profitable especially for tomatoes, until the 1960s, when mass production in Queensland and advances in overnight transport led to the decline of the industry. Some market gardens and now mostly derelict glasshouses still exist.

The track beside Narrabeen Lakes.

Mona Vale

Above Warriewood Beach from the Recreation Reserve on top of the headland separating Warriewood and Mona Vale Beach, there's a view of the beach, the Golf Course and in the distance Pittwater sparkles between the fold of hills on each side. Colourful paragliders sometimes take off from the Reserve and glide over the beach on the sea breeze.

Another worthwhile detour from Mona Vale is up to Mona Vale Headland Reserve for the view across Bongin Bongin Bay towards Mona Vale, Mona Vale Beach and Warriewood Beach. Bongin Bongin, the original name of Mona Vale, were the words Aborigines used to articulate the sound of muskets going off.

Adolph Albers

As you continue north on Barrenjoey Road you may spot some medieval battlements amongst the houses on the headland. This in Bungan Castle, built by Adolph Albers.

Pounding surf on the rock shelf at Turimetta.

Mullet Creek Warriewood.

Early morning surf at Warriewood.

Albers, a German migrant who arrived in Sydney in 1880 aged 14, was apprenticed to a Sydney art dealer, then went into business on his own. He represented more than 60 Australian artists over the years, many of them the best known artists of the day such as Sydney Long, Arthur Streeton and John Longstaff. On a journey to Pittwater in 1918 the cliff of Bungan Head caught Albers' eye and he decided it would be just the spot to build a house to resemble the medieval fortresses perched on rocky crags on the Rhine he remembered from his youth in Germany. The following year Albers bartered a Sydney Long painting for the headland site and commenced construction of his 'castle' from rock quarried close by. The story goes that Albers would invite his friends to the site for a weekend party, then set them to work on the house from plans drawn in the sand on nearby Bungan Beach. As a result the house, though comfortable inside, is rather roughly built in a mixture of Gothic, Norman and Saxon styles. Albers filled the house with his lifetimes' collection of works of art, antiquities and bric-a-brac, which he was always pleased to show to visitors. He lived at the house until he died in 1959. Though the castle remains, much of the original grounds have since been sub-divided and built on.

The headlands of the Northern Beaches seen from Turimetta Head.

Bungan Beach

Bungan Beach is never crowded even on the hottest summer days because it is only accessible by a steep track at the northern end off Bungan Head road. So unpatronised was the beach that it didn't have its own Life Saving Club until 1953. The Club's first shelter was a discarded Caterpillar tractor case.

Newport to Avalon

After passing Bungan Beach, Barrenjoey Road skirts Bushrangers Hill, then begins a long gentle descent to Newport Beach. For many years Newport Beach was known as 'Farrell's Beach'. John Farrell was an Irishman who arrived in Sydney in 1813 as a convict, transported for seven years for 'possession of an illegal bank note'. Granted a ticket of leave, Farrell saved enough money to purchase 'a certain farm of land containing thirty acres or thereabouts' in 1822 for '36 pounds, 10 shillings'. The farm, on Pittwater, was called 'Belgooler'. In the 1830s and 1840s Farrell received grants of 150 acres at Newport, including most of the land near the beach.

Warriewood Beach. At low tide you can walk around to Mona Vale Beach in the background.

John Farrell's grandson Johnny (the third) eventually inherited the farms in 1881. Johnny, among other things, worked as a contractor for the Roads Department and built the first bridges on Pittwater Road over Queenscliff Lagoon and Narrabeen Lakes.

Newport

Newport's development as a town took place because it was the shortest distance from Manly to the waterways of Pittwater and the Hawkesbury. This development was dependent on access via Pittwater Road and the provision of transport along it. The first exploratory journeys from Manly were undertaken to reach Pittwater to search for farming land in the vicinity of Broken Bay. Though there were pioneer settlers who established farms north of Manly and at Pittwater, access to the district remained difficult with no accommodation for travellers and supplies had to be carried.

So Pittwater and the Northern Beaches remained a remote seldom visited destination in the years to come. Land on the Pittwater side of Newport belonged to the descendants of William Wentworth (of Vaucluse House fame) and these estates were frozen and not allowed to be built on. This restriction on land sales was lifted by a special Act of Parliament in 1877 and land at Newport was bought by Charles Edward Jeannerett who ran a steamer service between Sydney and Parramatta. Jeannerett also built a hotel and pier on the Pittwater side of Newport, established a coach service to connect it with Manly and secured the mail contract to carry the post from the Hawkesbury to Manly. To service these activities he bought a small steamer to carry the mail and passengers from Gosford and the Broken Bay district to the 'New Port' as he called his fledgling settlement.

Traffic along Pittwater Road increased because for those travelling from the north of the state it was quicker to go from Gosford by water to Newport, coach to Manly, then ferry to Sydney than to take the circuitous inland route to Sydney on the Great North Road. In the early 1880's the Boulton family owned the Newport Hotel and ran their own coach service to Manly. Harry Boulton used to drive the coach, and in the afternoon when the guests had finished their drinks and were back in their seats, the parrot on the verandah used to squawk, 'All aboard Harry'.

By May 1889 William Woolcott of the Sydney Tourist Bureau wrote:

Mona Vale.

The Sunday congregation has just left the Bahai Temple at Mona Vale.

Ready to withstand a siege, Bungan castle on the centre of Bungan Head was built by an eccentric art dealer.

The number of passengers sent by this office over the Pittwater Road from Manly to Newport during the past two years is slightly in excess of 2,000 and the traffic shows an increase of between 50 and 75 per cent per annum.

Though tourists could often also expect a little exercise on the way. According to a report in the *Sydney Mail* in 1890, on the journey north from Manly:

> When coaches with a heavy load encountered stiff hills, the passengers were obliged to make the gradient on foot, the stretch, however, does one good, besides relieving the horses.

But far exceeding the number of tourists travelling by road were those that came by sea. In the 1890s day trips to Newport were organised carrying up to 1200 passengers on large chartered steamers sailing from Sydney through the heads to the wharf on the Pittwater side of Newport.

Newport by bus

The first motor omnibuses on the Manly to Newport run entered service in 1906. The buses of 'The Manly – Pittwater Omnibus Company Ltd' had seats for 16 passengers and drove at a top speed of 30 m.p.h., completing the 17 kilometre journey in 49 minutes, a saving of 40 minutes over the horse drawn carriage. However passengers found that they not only had to dismount for exercise, but were also expected to push if the bus expired on the way up Bushrangers Hill. That is if they got to their destination at all, because the bus frequently broke down completely. The buses were withdrawn after a short time because of insufficient patronage, to re-appear again – this time for good – in 1911.

Although there was an increase in visitors to Newport on holidays and weekends, it still remained a quiet little settlement overlooking Pittwater. In 1904 the population was only 100 and in a photo taken in 1912 you can count no more than 12 houses on the ocean side of Newport. The first telephone exchange opened at Newport in March 1914 with three subscribers, including the Newport Hotel. But this, as everything else, was on the Pittwater side. A map of 1924 illustrates the beach side of Newport as still all farms. It wasn't until 1928 that a post and telephone office opened next to Barrenjoey Road on the beach side. Various names were bandied about for the new office before someone hit on 'Newport Beach'. 'Farrell's Beach' apparently didn't get a mention, even though Johnny Farrell the third was still kicking and living on his Newport property.

Newport Surf Club

Newport Beach Surf Life Saving Club was one of the first in Australia, founded in 1911. In those days 70% of the ratepayers of Warringah, including Newport, were non-resident and many of the houses were weekenders. There weren't enough local surf lifesavers to patrol the beach during holidays, and their numbers were supplemented by outsiders, including

Bungan Beach with a typical summer afternoon crowd.

Fossils are often found among the rocks at the south end of Bungan Beach.

When Governor Phillip discovered Pittwater he described it as 'I think the finest piece of water I ever saw'.

A glimpse of Pittwater at Newport.

some hardy souls who used to cycle up for the day from Mosman. The Club was one of the first in Australia to have lady members, but the Surf Life Saving Association was a men only organisation so the Newport Ladies' Surf Club was formed. At the first surf carnivals there were no trailers to bring the surf life-saving boats by road so other clubs used to row to Newport for the occasion. That included Bondi, whose team used to row all the way to Newport then back again after a day's racing. The present clubhouse dates to 1933.

Bilgola

Continuing our journey north from Newport Beach swing around the headland and take the road called The Serpentine which winds down to Bilgola. The settlement sits at the base of a semi-tropical sheltered gully with the most extensive stands of cabbage tree palms still existing in the Sydney area. When James Meehan surveyed the district in 1814 he named it 'Belgoula' which was Aboriginal for 'swirling waters'. Then a local grazier, Mr R. Henderson, who later sold his farm on the other side of the hill to John Farrell, called it in the 1820s 'Belgooler'. On the 1904 map of shire boundaries it was called 'Bulgola' and sometime over the next 20 years the 'u' officially became an 'i'. The first 'Bilgola House', which at the time was literally the one and only house there, was built above the beach by the politician the Right Honourable William Dalley in about 1870. His son, John Bede Dalley (1876-1935) also lived at Bilgola and was a writer of satirical novels. Writers must like the location because Morris West, who penned many novels including 'The Devil's Advocate' and 'The Salamander' lived here. So too did Thomas Keneally.

The Serpentine winds like a serpent through the pines behind the beach then leads to a lookout on Bilgola Head. This area was saved from development because 75 acres at Bilgola Head were made a Defence Reserve in 1884. Though it doesn't look as if it was ever fortified. However, it's a good bastion from which to enjoy the views of Newport and Avalon.

Reverend John Therry

The coal bore was an enterprise of the Reverend John Therry who, since coal had been discovered at Newcastle and Wollongong, was convinced the seam ran in a continuous line beneath the coast. Therry, born in Ireland, arrived in Australia in 1820 with the honour of being the first and 'only Roman Catholic priest for … the whole of the continent'; although for practical purposes his 'parish' covered the east coast from Melbourne to Brisbane. In the early days of the penal settlement practice of the Catholic faith wasn't encouraged as any gathering of Irish convicts was seen as a prelude to sedition, but Therry was warmly received by Macquarie who granted him the site for St Mary's Cathedral in Sydney and, promised him 'all the land between Narrabeen Lakes and McCarr's Creek at Pittwater. Therry was stripped of his post of the Catholic chaplain by Governor Darling, but reinstated by Governor Bourke who belatedly made good Macquarie's promise of land on the north shore. In August 1833 Bourke granted Therry 1200 acres on the peninsular between Pittwater and the Pacific Ocean at an annual rent of £9 8s 4d with a condition that it couldn't be sold for five years and 85 acres must be placed under cultivation. With a further grant of 280 acres Therry received in 1837 his holdings covered almost the entire peninsular from Newport to Whale Beach including Avalon and Bilgola beaches – property which in today's terms would be worth well in excess of a billion dollars.

He christened ground around Careel Bay 'Josephtown' where he intended a city would one day rise for which he had plans for a school, court house and cathedral. This project was to be financed by the extraction of coal which Therry was enthusiastically searching for. He worked for years looking for coal at Avalon at the expense of thousands of pounds before finally giving up the project. Josephtown never got off the ground although some of the men who worked on Therry's coal bore stayed in the district, lived in huts and grew fruit and vegetables, and when they died were buried in the cemetery at Careel Bay. Therry passed on in 1864, relegated to the post of parish priest of Balmain, and was buried in St Mary's, the cathedral he founded. The following year the cathedral burnt to the ground and the finance for the construction of a new cathedral was raised through the sale of Therry's land on the Northern Beaches which he had left to the Jesuit order.

Avalon

Avalon was such a long way north of Manly that it remained for many years native bushland populated by kangaroos. A typical picture, taken in 1906, shows just four houses at Avalon with the bush behind traversed by the white band of the unsealed Barrenjoey Road lined by telegraph poles. Substantial land holdings in the district were held by Arthur Small, who

The ferry wharf at Snapperman Beach.

Scotland Island seen from the ferry.

Careel Bay and Stokes Point, Pittwater.

wished to sub-divide and develop his estate but still retain the bush character of the area. Small began land sales at 'Avalon' in 1921 of blocks of a minimum of 60 metres deep and 20 metres wide, imposing a covenant on the bill of sale preventing unnecessary destruction of trees and banning the owner from further subdivision of the block. Lots were sold for £100 each with two year's free membership of the local golf club.

Whale Beach

The story of development at Whale Beach is typical of the rest of the peninsular. Originally no one wanted it. When the Napper Estate at Whale Beach was first sub-divided and put up for sale at the turn of the century not one block at Whale Beach sold. In the 1940s building blocks went for under 200 pounds, while these days it's not unusual to see completed homes sold for over $1 million.

Whale Beach is known, according to a recent newspaper article, as being home 'to the rich, famous and eccentric'. Some of these 'rich, famous and eccentric' people enthusiastically assist at the biggest fund raising event for the local surf club, the annual Miss Whale Beach Quest, started in 1947 and open to all-comers. They sit at the judging, and 'rich, famous and eccentric' local ladies have also been glad to lend a hand recently with the addition of the 'Mr Whale Beach' contest.

Visitors to Sydney have been making the pilgrimage to Palm Beach ever since Phillip led the first expedition here in March 1788. Phillip travelled north from Sydney in a long boat and cutter and was the first to record the name of the headland which he christened 'Barrenjuee', apparently after an Aboriginal word for a 'young kangaroo'.

The Customs Station

The Palm Beach district remained a sparsely settled wilderness inhabited by the odd fisherman or vegetable gardener until 1843 when the Customs Station was established just south of Barrenjoey Headland. There were many blatant cases of smuggling known to be taking place in Brisbane Waters and it prompted the authorities to establish the permanent Customs Station at Barrenjoey. The Customs Officer had assistance to carry out his duties

Newport from the little park above the beach.

Newport Surf Club.

Surfers at Newport.

Boats of the Royal Motor Yacht Club and Royal Prince Alfred Yacht Club at Newport.

Bilgola Beach.

Palmgrove Park Avalon.

Avalon Beach.

of coastal surveillance, a typical return of annual expenses for the Station detailing the Custom Officer's salary of £250 (a generous stipend to ensure no temptation to graft), coxswain 2s 6d a day, 5 convict boatmen at 6d a day, 6 rations a day 1s 4d , two suits of clothing for five men at £2 each, a total of £448. Life settled into a routine for the Customs Officer or 'Coast Waiter' at the isolated outpost of Barrenjoey. As well as their daily duties there was a vegetable garden to attend to and the family needs, because the Coast Waiters brought their wives and children to live at the station.

Alexander Ross, Coast Waiter from 1854-1868, crafted several effergies of soldiers and mounted them at strategic points on the sand spit and headland to frighten off smugglers. Albert Black who succeeded Ross in 1868, was Coast Waiter for 22 years. His duties, for each of which he received a salary, included Coast Waiter, Telegraph Master, Post Master and an Assistant Inspector for the Fisheries Commission. The station was connected to the outside world when a telegraph line was laid in 1870. Black was the first Telegraph Station Master, and in August the following year also became the local Postmaster when the 'Barrenjoey Post Office' opened at the Station.

Black never hesitated to row out to any ship in distress, and when the schooner *Resolute* ran aground in a storm on West Head near the beach which now carries its name, it was Black who rowed across Pittwater to save the crew.

In the 1870s an average of 370 ships a year sailed through Broken Bay and up the Hawkesbury to Windsor, but the trade declined with the silting up of the river during the drought of the 1880s, and by the 1890s the railway had taken much of the river traffic. There was no need anymore for a Customs Station and it closed in 1903. The handsome stone buildings were periodically rented as holiday homes until being maliciously destroyed by fire in 1976.

Nature's sculpture on Bilgola Plateau.

Barrenjoey Lighthouse

Since the 1850s a warning light had been placed in the window of a hut on the headland in rough weather. Then in 1868 the 'Stewart Towers' were erected on the east and west side of the headland that each threw a light about three miles. They were named after Mr Robert Stewart, M.P. for East Sydney, who agitated for the erection of a permanent light on the headland. With the increasing volume of coastal traffic entering Broken Bay a more powerful, taller, single light was required and the authorities requested the Colonial Architect, James Barnet, to design one. Barnet was familiar with the site as he had designed new stone cottages at the Customs House. Barrenjoey, with its matchless setting, was Barnet's favourite lighthouse of the many he designed. All the materials for the construction of the lighthouse except the stone itself, which was quarried on site, were hauled up the escarpment on a trolley track. Utzon, the Sydney Opera House architect, used to have a studio at Palm Beach and thought the assistant-keeper's cottage of undressed sandstone was his favourite building in Australia as each block was different 'They are all like original oil paintings'. The foundation stone for the lighthouses was laid on 15th April 1880 and the building was completed 15 months later.

The first lighthouse keeper was George Mulhall (born 1814) who had attended the light in the Stewart Towers. At that time the lighthouse keepers lived in cottages at the site of the present day Palm Beach Golf links and walked along the peninsular and up the hill by the Customs Station path to attend the lights.

Until the road was built to Barrenjoey, all supplies came by steamer. The keepers grew their own vegetables, had peach and apricot trees in the cottage courtyards and had fresh eggs, meat and milk from ducks, chickens, cows and goats they kept. The nearest hospital was at Manly, so most deliveries were home births. Altogether over 50 children were born at the lighthouse and Customs Station.

Although it was an isolated posting at Barrenjoey, it was never a lonely one, because there were sometimes three families at the lighthouse and three at the Customs Station. With so many children of school age a decision was made to establish a school. Known as the Barrenjoey Provisional School, it was the first school north of Manly and opened in 1871 in a boatman's cottage at Chinaman's Beach (Snapperman Beach). By the following year there were 24 pupils attending.

When the Customs Station closed in 1903, the business of transmitting and receiving telegrams and running the local telephone exchange (which was transferred to the lighthouse) fell to the lighthouse keeper. Palm Beach locals who didn't have their own phone had an energetic walk up to the lighthouse if they wished to make a public call. A

Bangalley Head, accessible by a walking track, is the highest point on Sydney's Northern Beaches.

A view looking north. Careel Bay is on the left, Whale Beach on the right, and Palm Beach at the end of the peninsula.

Avalon Beach looking towards Bangalley Head.

Tree ferns in Horden Park. A track cuts through the park from Florida Road to the south end of Palm Beach.

Whale Beach. No one can quite remember what the whale had to do with it.

Previous pages: Barrenjoey Lighthouse and Palm Beach.

The Bible Garden on Mitchell Road contains plants that occur in the Holyland.

Looking towards Palm Beach from Snapperman Beach.

The view of Palm Beach from above Pittwater.

Barrenjoey Lighthouse.

The paved track to Barrenjoey.

The south end of Palm Beach is still marked on maps as 'Cabbage Tree Boat Harbour'.

Barrenjoey Headland, like a hammer-head shark about to strike.

A grove of palms in Wiltshire Park.

telephone exchange opened in Palm Beach village in 1920, and the exchange at the lighthouse closed, to the great relief of the lighthouse keepers and their wives who had found the duty required 'constant attendance night and day'.

In 1932 the light at Barrenjoey Lighthouse was converted from kerosene to automatic acetylene operation, increasing its power from 700 candles to 6,000 candles. That year a Commonwealth notice advised mariners 'The Lightkeepers have been withdrawn and the light is now unwatched'. The closing reference in the visitors' book stated the Lightkeepers had left and 'no person was on the Station for the first time since the light was first established in 1868 ... a period of 64 years'. The lighthouse was converted to an electric powered 1,000 watt tungsten lamp in 1972 with an output of 75,000 candlepower and a geographical range of 26 nautical miles. The lightkeeper's cottages were neglected and soon became derelict, but were later restored by tenants.

Settlement of Palm Beach

Though there was plenty of activity in the early days at the Customs Station and Lighthouse, the rest of the peninsular remained virtually deserted. In 1912 when an auction of 88 newly sub-divided blocks took place, it was easier to bring prospective patrons by ferry from Newport to a wharf at Snapperman Beach than it was over the rough track along the peninsular. Raine and Horne advertised the land sale as the 'Barrenjoey Palm Beach Estate' the first known reference to Palm Beach and the name that was adopted for the suburb.

The road to Palm Beach was upgraded for cars in 1920, but even then people didn't flock to the district. There was no road on the beach side. In October 1938 the 190 bus service was established from Wynyard to Palm Beach. The 40 kilometre route run by the double-deckers was (and still is) the longest in metropolitan Sydney and takes an hour and a quarter traffic permitting. During the War it was thought the double-deckers may need

to carry soldiers to the peninsular to repel the Japanese invasion, and they were painted in camouflage and the windows replaced by shutters. The buses on the 190 route were the last double-deckers operating in Sydney because the new long articulated buses of the Urban Transit Authority couldn't get round the Bilgola bends. The double-deckers were withdrawn from service when the bends were widened in 1986.

The walk to the Lighthouse

From the Seaplane Wharf on Barrenjoey Beach, five minutes walk north on the beach takes you to the base of the headland and the track that leads to the lighthouse. This path, recently upgraded by the National Parks and Wildlife Service, is the original path cut by the convicts for the Customs officers to reach their lookout. For the twenty minute walk to the top of the headland my recommendation would be take the customs trail on the way up and to return by the broad track leading directly west from the lighthouse. This second track was built to haul supplies up the hill to the lighthouse and lightkeepers' cottages by horse and cart. It's still paved in places with the original sandstone slabs.

Dark Gully on Barrenjoey Road.

The Blue Mountains

The most famous view in the Mountains, The Three Sisters from Echo Point.

The Blue Mountains

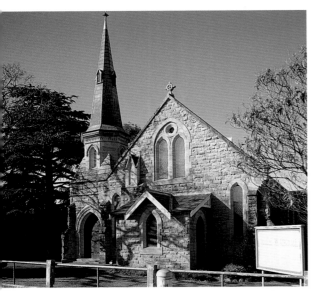

Frazer Memorial Church, Springwood.

The Blue Mountains National Park, less than two hours drive from Sydney, has some of the most dramatic scenery and some of the best walks to be found anywhere in Australia.

For thousands of years, Aboriginal people of the Daruk and Gundungara tribes lived in parts of the Blue Mountains and travelled through them to other areas for ceremonial reasons. Hand stencils, axe-grinding grooves, rock carvings, water holes, and shelter caves remain. Occupation sites have been found at Glenbrook, Hawkesbury Heights, Kings Tableland and the Megalong Valley.

Governor Phillip wrote in a letter to Lord Sydney in 1790 that 'native fires are frequently seen on the tops of the mountains, where the air in winter must be very sharp'. The explorer Francis Barrallier travelled with an Aboriginal guide named Gogy, and met Gundungara people on the southern side of the Mountains. Later explorers saw bark huts and fires, but no people. Some might have been hiding, but many Aborigines might have already died of introduced diseases.

Early Western explorers

In 1789 Governor Phillip and his party rowed up the Hawkesbury River. At the junction with the Grose River, Phillip named the Carmarthen Hills (Kurrajong and beyond) and the Landsdowne Hills (Lapstone and beyond). He declared that he wanted 'shortly, to explore their summits', little knowing how difficult this would prove to be.

For over twenty years people tried to cross the Mountains, without success. Their aims included adventure, scientific discovery and pastoral expansion. Caley wrote to Sir Joseph Banks that 'botany is not the primary object but…an enthusiastic pride of going farther than any person has yet been'. He found thirty new plants but complained 'The roughness of the country I found beyond description'.

In 1789 William Dawes followed a direct compass course towards Round Hill (Mount Hay), reaching a point northwest of Linden. George Bass accompanied by the intrepid Henry Hacking tried travelling on the southern side of the Mountains towards Kanangra Plateau. The soldier-explorer William Paterson travelled up the Grose River, and John Wilson, an ex-convict, was sent on an expedition with Irish convicts to bring back the message that China was *not* just over the Mountains, a common belief at the time.

The lure of discovery was blunted by a ruling forbidding military personnel from leaving their posts to carry out exploratory expeditions. To circumvent this, in 1802 Governor King appointed an ensign in the N.S.W. Corps, Francis Barrallier, to the 'vice-regal staff' and 'sent him on an embassy to the King of the Mountains'. However Barrallier curtailed his diplomatic mission after getting lost in the Kowmung River valley west of Picton. After several efforts to scale this seemingly impenetrable barrier King was prompted to write, 'As far as respects the extension of agriculture beyond the first range of mountains, that is an idea that must be given up…'.

The first successful crossing

Eventually, it was a free settler, Gregory Blaxland, who lived with his brother on a farm at Newington near Parramatta who led the first successful crossing of the Blue Mountains in 1813. Blaxland had a personal incentive for discovering new grazing country, having suffered heavy stock losses in the drought of 1812. He also already possessed some knowledge of the country west of Sydney, having accompanied Governor Macquarie in an exploration of the Warragamba River in 1811 and being informed by other explorers of the course of the Grose River. Blaxland surmised that the ridge providing the watershed between two rivers could serve as a track leading into the heart of the mountains and across them. His plan was once he'd ascended the ridge 'being careful not to cross any of [the streams] but to go round their sources' in so doing 'keeping the heads of the gulleys… on their left hand, and… the River Grose on their right.' To accompany him on the expedition, Blaxland invited his neighbour William Charles Wentworth of Homebush and William Lawson, who brought his surveying skills with him and later became Commandant

A convict-built stone bridge at Glenbrook is the oldest on the Australian mainland.

The track through Sassafras Gully.

Some boulder-hopping is required to walk through Glenbrook Gorge.

A section of the Terrace Falls Track.

Mossy rocks on the Terrace Falls Track.

Terrace Falls.

National Pass, Wentworth Falls.

over the area west of Mount York. Blaxland wrote of Wentworth and Lawson, 'I have to express my thanks for their company, and to acknowledge, that without their assistance, I should have had but little chance of success.' The expedition left Gregory Blaxland's farm at the South Creek (Duck River) on 11th May 1813, 'attended by four servants, with five dogs, and four horses laden with provisions, ammunition and other necessaries.'

According to Blaxland's account, written in the third person ten years later, they had to cut and carry grass for the horses and sometimes 'had to fetch water up the side of the precipice, about six hundred feet high, and could get scarcely enough for the party.' Pushing on through the 'death-like stillness of the interior' interrupted only by the howling of dingoes at night, they had difficulty persuading their convict servants to continue to march once they were a few days out. They could see 'The natives, as observed by the smoke of their fires' moving in front of them and at one night's camp 'they had reason to believe... that they had been in great danger; that the natives had followed their track, and advanced on them in the night, intending to have speared them by the light of their fire, but that the dogs drove them off.' When they could they killed kangaroo, which they found 'very acceptable' as a change from salt meat, but were surprised that at 'night the frost covered the ground very thick and froze the leg of a kangaroo quite through.' Three weeks out, after having frequently to hack their way through the bush for themselves and their horses, they reached a hill 'in the shape of a sugarloaf' which they climbed to be greeted with a view of 'forest or grassland, sufficient in extent... to support the stock of the Colony for the next thirty years.' The hill was Mt Blaxland, west of the Jenolan Caves turnoff. Having 'marked out, a road by which the passage of the mountain might easily be effected' and with 'their provisions... nearly expended' and 'the whole party ill with bowel complaints' they resolved 'to return home by the track they came' and reached the safety of their homes on the 6th of June 'all in good health'. For their trail blazing expedition across the mountains each of the explorers received a grant of 1,000 acres from Macquarie in the new country.

Surveying the new route

Later that year Macquarie despatched the surveyor George William Evans to confirm the route and the existence of fertile land on the other side. Evans had migrated to Sydney via the Cape of Good Hope and worked as surveyor-general and as a storekeeper before being dismissed for fraud in 1805. Anxious to redeem himself, Evans assembled two assistants and three convicts and on 20th November set out on the route pioneered by Blaxland. Surveying the passage on the way, they reached Mt Blaxland in eight days, descended onto the Western Plains and pushed into the country 100 miles beyond the point reached by Blaxland, Lawson and Wentworth. Evans was effusive in his praise of the new territory reporting vast plains 'equal to every demand which this colony may have for an extension of tillage and pasture lands for a century to come' surpassing 'in beauty and fertility of soil, any... seen in New South Wales, or Van Dieman's Land.' Though he cautioned

> I beg to observe that it will be impossible to drive cattle, or attempt sending a cart until the road is made, for the reasons that the stumps and brush and sharp granite rocks will run into their feet and lame them.

After an expedition of seven weeks Evans returned on 8th January 1814. The surveyor and his companions were all rewarded with substantial land grants and the convicts granted conditional pardons and a small portion of land.

Building the road

Another William, William Cox, a former Lieutenant and Paymaster in the N.S.W. Corps and chief magistrate at Windsor offered his services to Macquarie to supervise construction of the road. For the task Cox gathered thirty convicts known to be 'well inclined hardy men who had been some years in the colony and accustomed to field labour' with a guard of eight soldiers and a smith to 'lay steel' and sharpen axes. Macquarie's instructions to Cox were

> The road is to commence at the ford on the river Nepean, and from thence across the Blue Mountains to the Macquarie River... [and] Bathurst Plains... The road thus made must be at least 12ft wide, so as to permit two carts or other wheel carriages to pass each other with ease... Any small bridges... must be 12ft wide... where it can with ease and convenience be done, I should prefer the road to be made 16ft wide.

So that Cox would not be disturbed by idle sightseers coming to view the work Macquarie issued an instruction that no person was to cross the Nepean without a pass signed by him personally. Construction of the road commenced in the midst of winter, the following

The road to Terrace Falls.

Happiness is... a cuddle at the top of Wentworth Falls.

Rugged sandstone escarpments in the Grose Valley.

excerpts from Cox's diary detailing progress.

July 22 One of the fellers, W. Lonian, received a hurt in the face and shoulder through the limb of a tree falling on him.

Aug 2 The workmen go on with much cheerfulness, and do their work well. Gave them a quantity of cabbage as a present.

Aug 5 Timber both thick and heavy, with a thick, strong brush, the roots of which are very hard to grub up, making it altogether extremely hard work.

Aug 6 ... measured the new road and found we had completed nine miles... The men all healthy and cheerful.

Aug 11 Clear weather. The wind very strong from the west, made it dangerous in falling the timber... The smith set up his forge; employed in repairing tools

Aug 17 The timber... very tall and thick. Measured a dead tree which we felled that was 81ft to the first branch, and a blood tree 15ft 6in in circumference.

Aug 26 ... arrived at Martin's, where I found the sergeant of the party, he having died the day before. Sent to Windsor to the sergeant commanding there for a coffin... Wrote to the Governor for another sergeant.

Aug 29 Commenced operations on the mountain, with all the men... Had to remove an immense quantity of rock, both in going up the mountain and on the pass leading to the bluff on the west of it... The men worked extremely hard and smart today.

Sept 12 The bridge we have completed is 80ft long, 15ft wide at one end and 12ft at the other' 35ft of it is planked, the remainder filled up with stones... It is now complete – a strong, solid bridge, and will, I have no doubt, be reckoned a good-looking one by travellers that pass through the mountain.

Sept 24 Wrote to the Governor for a further supply of gunpowder, to enable us to blow up the rocks in our way...

Sept 30 Rain until about 5 o'clock in the evening... Blankets belonging to the men very wet and uncomfortable.

Nov 3 ... went forward... to examine the mountain at the end of the ridge... Found it much worse than I expected... the hill is so very steep about half-a-mile down that it is not possible to make a good road... without going to a very great expense. I have, therefore, made up my mind to make such a road as a cart can go down empty or with a very light load... and such a road will also answer to drive stock down to the forest ground... no produce can be brought from thence to headquarters except for bullocks or sheep. The sheep will also be able to bring their fleeces up and be shorn on the mountains...

Nov 5 The blacksmith made eight pikes for self-defence against the natives. Lewis and a party took the dogs down to the forest ground. Killed a fine kangaroo; weighs about 120lb.

Nov 14 Sick list : F. Dwyer, cold, pains in limbs; S. Freeman, cold and swelled face; S.Crook, cold, bad eyes; V. Hanragan, cold, pains in limbs; S. Walters, hurt by bullock. The extreme wet weather we had a fortnight before we arrived here has given most of the men colds, but as they are now dry lodged, and in addition to their large ration, have fresh kangaroo at least three times a week, it is to be hoped they will soon recover.

Cox's gang completed the work in six months. By any yardstick it was an incredible achievement. Starting at the ford on the Nepean at close to sea-level the road climbed to a height of 3,500 feet as it wound up and over the mountains to Bathurst 101 miles away, crossing on the way more than 12 creeks spanned by wooden bridges. For their part in the enterprise the convict workers were rewarded with their freedom.

Macquarie's trip across the mountains

To open the road Governor Macquarie and his wife travelled across the mountains by carriage with an entourage of 10 others including Cox, Evans, his aide de camp, Major Henry Anthill who wrote a journal on the 'excursion' and Mr Lewin the artist who rendered sketches on the way to record the event for posterity. Accompanying them were five baggage-carts, about 40 servants and a number of cattle. Leaving on 25th April 1815, after ascending the first range they stopped at 3 o'clock that afternoon for their first camp, Anthill describing how

We found all our baggage, caravans, and servants safely arrived before us, and drawn up in regular order to receive us, which they did with three cheers. Our dinner being ready and a table spread in the open air, we soon sat down to partake of it... After dinner, served out a dram of rum to every man, which they were to receive every day, and all appeared happy and contented... Our party was formed into different groups, each having a large fire of its own, without which, from the coldness of the nights at this season of the year, it would be impossible to sleep in comfort. These different fires had, from the background where I was, a very beautiful effect, and enabled me to observe the scene before me. Some were busily employed cooking, others were making their huts or cutting down timber for fuel, and

Sylvia Falls, the Valley of the Waters.

This cliff track above Wentworth Falls leads to the National Pass.

Mist fills the Jamison Valley. Photographed close to Queen Victoria Lookout, Wentworth Falls.

Garlands of bark hang from a gum tree, Wentworth Falls.

reminded me by their various occupations of what I had read of a camp of gypsies or the bivouacs of a Continental army. I remained here a short time and then retired to rest for the night in my hammock, swung between two poles and covered with a tarpaulin, by the side of a comfortable fire large enough to roast an ox.

… I rose at daylight and began to get part of the baggage off… Before we left the ground, the Governor and Mrs Macquarie… walked down to the spring where we had been supplied with water, situated about a mile down a deep glen… From this spring and surrounding forest, the Governor gave the name of Spring Wood to this station.

Three days later:

About 11 o'clock, at the 49-mile tree, we came to the pass down the mountain into the new country below… This pass had been made with great labour down a very steep mountain of upwards of 600 feet… It was with much difficulty and exertion we got the carts down by fixing drag-ropes behind and holding on with the people. It was so perpendicular in places that the cattle could scarcely keep their footing. We, however, in about two hours' hard work, got them all down in safety… we moved on… to our station on the banks of a small stream, which the Governor called Cox's River… The hill itself was called Mount York… and the valley which we rode through to Fox's River the Vale of Clwyd, through its resemblance to a place of that name in Wales.

The excursion arrived at the 'Grand Depot, Bathurst Plains' on 4th May nine days after setting out. On Sunday 7th 'the British flag was displayed for the first time in this new country' and Macquarie 'then named the place and new town to be marked out, "Bathurst", and each drank a bumper, some in wine and the rest in rum, to the King's health, and success to the town.'

Cox's observation that sheep would have to carry the wool on their backs up the pass at Mt York proved to be true, and a woolshed for sheep-shearing was established at Blackheath. It wasn't until the less severe Victoria Pass was opened on the western descent of the mountains in 1832 that a cart carrying any kind of load was able to make the ascent.

The conquering of the ridge on the east side of the mountains proved difficult too, roads up Lapstone Hill were built by Cox, Lawson (1824), and Mitchell (1834). They met at the Pilgrim Inn (c1825) in Blaxland, the ruins of which can be seen at the McDonalds.

The naturalist Charles Darwin during his visit to Australia in 1836 travelled up

One of the prettiest sights in the Mountains, Sylvia Falls, the Valley of the Waters.

Mitchell's Pass and wrote 'The ascent is not steep, the road having been cut with much care on the side of a sandstone cliff'. Sophia Stanger travelled to Bathurst with her husband and five children in 1841. Their dray got stuck on Lapstone Hill, and 'here we must have stayed had not a number of men forming the iron-gang (who were returning from their work of improving these roads) kindly assisted us, for a small sum of money to buy themselves tobacco.' The travellers walked and helped with the dray. Stanger wrote:

> Through this day poor Eliza walked on with dear baby, and I brought up the rear, and blocked the wheels at every stoppage, sometimes left half-a-mile behind, and then having to run as fast as possible to perform this new but somewhat irksome duty.

Spring in Leura.

Bell's Line of Road

The route from Kurrajong to Bell was discovered in 1823 by teenager Archibald Bell, who learnt of it from an Aborigine. Louisa Atkinson noted in the 1860s that the road 'is a great thoroughfare of the cattle and sheep which supply the Sydney markets'. It was upgraded for security reasons during the Second World War and was later sealed, thus becoming a popular alternative route to Sydney.

The railway

Until the development of the railway there was very little settlement in the Mountains apart from innkeepers and toll-collectors. Stations opened at the Weatherboard (Wentworth Falls) and Blackheath in 1867 and at 'The Crushers' platform in Katoomba in 1874. The construction of the Zig-Zag railway at Clarence solved the problem of getting the railway line down the Mountains. Govett's Leap and Wentworth Falls were the first accessible scenic areas as they were near public railway platforms.

Modern travel up the Mountains

As you approach the Blue Mountains by car you see the hills through their famous blue haze – caused by droplets of eucalyptus oil in the air evaporated from the gum forests. After the Penrith turnoff from the M4 motorway you rise up the Lapstone Monocline to the plateau of the mountains. The first town on the highway is Glenbrook. From here it is a steady rise to Mount Victoria, the highest town in the Mountains. This is much the same route as that followed by the early explorers Blaxland, Wentworth, and Lawson. From Mount Victoria you can take a side trip down the other side to Hartley and Jenolan Caves, or head to Richmond and Windsor through Kurrajong on the much less populated Bell's Line of Road.

Pools worn by small boulders in a creek-bed.

If you approach by train you will leave Emu Plains station and rise up to Lapstone. The trains are crucial for many Mountain residents who commute to the city for work. Fast electric double-decker trains leave regularly from Central Railway Station, Sydney. Trains are a great way to see the mountains as most of the attractions are a short walk from a station.

Lapstone

The Lapstone Monocline – the slope that marks the start of the Mountains – was formed when the Hawkesbury sandstone of the Sydney Basin was uplifted during the late Tertiary Period. The name Lapstone comes from the water-worn stones found here that looked like stones held by cobblers on their laps to beat leather against.

On Lapstone Hill on the old Great Western Highway there's an obelisk commemorating the work of John Whitton, engineer-in-chief of the New South Wales Railways from 1857 to 1889, and the ruins of No.1 Gatekeepers Cottage, built for the controller of the level crossing. John Whitton was responsible for the Great Western Railway, including the zigzags up the hills at each end of the Mountains which were considered marvels of engineering at the time.

At the top of the Lapstone monocline on the freeway after the big arrow warning signs, turn right into Knapsack Street and park at the end. This is the start of the Lapstone Zig-Zag walk. It follows an old cutting for the railway line and leads to the private platform built, at his own expense, by Sir John Lucas of Lucasville. There is a lookout at the end from which you can see Knapsack Viaduct, built in 1867, and used at times for both the railway line and the road and now carrying a humble bush track.

Glenbrook – Gateway to the Blue Mountains

Glenbrook is the tourist centre of the lower Blue Mountains. The Information Centre on the highway is open seven days (9am to 5pm weekdays; 8.30am to 4.30pm weekends).

Rainforest scenery on the track leading to Katoomba Falls.

The Scenic Skyway offers dramatic views of Katoomba Falls and the Three Sisters.

Members of the Messent tribe and friends near the Three Sisters.

Brochures and help are available, and books and souvenirs are sold. An invaluable free reference sheet produced by the Blue Mountains Tourism Authority is called 'Bushwalks in the Blue Mountains'. It lists 42 of the best Mountains walks on one side, with the name of the walk, the time taken at average walking pace, the grade (easy, medium or hard) and the highlights of that particular walk including whether there are views, waterfalls, rainforest and ferns on the way. The other side has a map with the locations of the walks. Most of the Mountains' towns straddle the Great Western Highway, spread out like knots on a rope. The steps at the Glenbrook Information Centre show this graphically. The Glenbrook Village Craft Market is held in the Community Hall beside the cinema on the first Sunday of the month from 9am to 4pm.

The Blue Mountains National Park includes more than 240,000 hectares of rugged bushland. It adjoins Wollemi National Park to the north and Kanangra-Boyd National Park to the south-west.

To get into the National Park at Glenbrook take the first left turn after the Information Centre into Ross Street, then turn left at the end of the shops into Burfitt Parade which becomes Bruce Road. The National Parks and Wildlife Centre here is open on weekends to give information and sell booklets about local walks. Next to the car park at the Centre a track leads down into the spectacular Glenbrook Gorge. This is now the route taken by the railway up the eastern escarpment of the Mountains and the occasional sight of a train passing high up on the side of the gorge seems strange in this tranquil setting.

A 7km drive into the National Park takes you to Euroka Clearing, a grassy car-camping area (book through the Richmond NPWS office) ideal for groups of kids to run around in. Euroka Clearing is a depression with relatively rich soil left from the erosion of a volcanic pipe. The Daruk people camped here, and stone axes dating back 12 to 15 thousand years have been found. Grey kangaroos, introduced to the area in 1968, browse at the edge of the clearing at dusk. Avoid the aggressive bull kangaroo.

The Glenbrook section of the National Park also has abseiling spots, natural swimming pools, and an Aboriginal hand stencil site at Red Hands Cave (8km, 4 hours, easy walk), found during a search for a lost child.

Blaxland

Turn right at the traffic lights at the McDonalds, go under the railway bridge and through the roundabout, take the first turn on the left and follow Mitchell's Pass to Lennox Bridge. This is the oldest bridge on the mainland, designed by David Lennox in 1833. Return to Blaxland or take the one way road to Emu Plains. This takes you to the cottage ruins and obelisk on part of the old Great Western Highway that was recently superseded by the motorway.

Warrimoo

Dorothy Wall, the author of the much-loved Blinky Bill books, lived at 3 Albert Street, Warrimoo. She was a single mother, and relied on the sale of her books to support herself and her child Peter, the prototype for the mischievous Blinky Bill. Peter went to Blaxland Public School. His classroom, built in 1926, is visible through the trees from the Great Western Highway.

In *Blinky Bill Grows Up*, Wall described Florabella Pass, which starts at the end of Florabella Street, writing 'Down in the gully hidden from view by tall gum-trees, banksias, and tea-trees, right against a huge rock the bazaar was held'. Jim Smith, author of several books on the Blue Mountains, describes this as 'the best walk in the lower Blue Mountains'. Look for *Lambertia formosa* (known as Mountain Devil because of its small horned fruits) and waratahs in spring. Listen for swamp wallabies, which sometimes visit residents' gardens. Use a tropical strength insect repellent to avoid leeches, and salt to remove them. Take the sign posted path on the left to return via Ross Crescent, Blaxland. You can do a car swap, walk or catch a train back to Warrimoo.

The railway line from Valley Heights to Katoomba covers 32km of the steepest railway line in Australia, climbing 695m. Two steam locomotives were coupled at the front and a 'pusher' worked at the rear to get the trains up the slope.

Springwood – First Mountains settlement

Springwood is the major town in the lower Blue Mountains. To get to the shopping centre turn left off the highway at the signs. To go to Winmalee and Hawkesbury Heights you also turn left here, then right at the first roundabout to cross the highway.

Katoomba Falls.

A grove of tree ferns near Federal Pass on the walk to the Ruined Castle.

The track leading to the Golden Stairs which climb from Federal Pass to Narrowneck.

You can walk between Springwood and Faulconbridge along Sassafras Creek, a pleasant forested gully. Start at Wiggins Track (off Yondell Road) or Sassafras Gully Road. Turn right at Sassafras Creek onto Victory Track. Exit past Clarinda Falls to the east of Faulconbridge Station.

Faulconbridge

Turn right off the highway into Grose Road to see the house where Norman Lindsay lived and worked, now a National Trust Museum. Paintings, etchings, ship models, and puppets from the Magic Pudding story are on display. The landscaped gardens with fountains and statues created by Lindsay can be seen on evening spotlight walks. Norman Lindsay also lived for a while at Everton House, now a restaurant on your right after the Faulconbridge shops.

Sir Henry Parkes, long term Premier of the NSW colony, bought 500 acres in Faulconbridge (his mother's maiden name) in 1876, opening his own railway platform in 1877. His grave is to the south of the railway station. Just west of his grave is the Corridor of Oaks, where an oak tree has been planted for each Australian Prime Minister.

At Linden, the next settlement in the mountains, turn left onto Tollgate Road and follow the signs across the highway and railway to King's Cave. This is a large cave that was used by The King's Own Regiment guarding convict road-builders. There are also stories of a bushranger called King who killed a man called Donohue, whose grave is nearby.

Woodford – Heart of the Mountains

Turn right from the highway at the 'Bull's Camp' sign to a picnic area with toilets and shelters, and an off-leash exercise area for dogs. Captain John Bull of the 99th Regiment formed a camp of fifty soldiers and prisoners here in 1842 to repair and upgrade the original road. An early observer described the scene:

> The Commandant's house is backed against the bush, overlooking the cantonments of his detachments and the huts of the prisoners under his orders. The barracks and convict boxes form a little hamlet of some two dozen buildings of whitewashed slabs with tall stone chimneys laid out on a rock plateau cleared of trees and commanding a prospect of melancholy and desolate sterility.

Walk along the grass at the west of the picnic area and down the rocky outcrop to a large 'room' carved into the rock, believed to have been a powderstore or convict cell. Further

north at the 'Flogging rock' sign there is a rock with parallel grooves – perhaps to allow blood to flow away after a whipping?

Woodford Academy, the oldest group of buildings in the Mountains, is on the right of the highway. This National Trust building, open to the public from 10am to 4pm on the third Saturday of each month was built as the Woodman's Inn in the 1830s and was extended to serve the gold rush trade. The hotel was altered in 1868 to convert it into a home for Sir Alfred Fairfax, who worked for his uncle at the *Sydney Morning Herald*. John MacManamey later established a boys' school there.

Woodford was one site from which the Transit of Venus was viewed in 1874. Alfred Fairfax, an amateur astronomer, took part in the scientific exercise, the aim of which was to make measurements to help calculate the distance of the earth from the sun. This had also been one of the aims of Cook's first voyage in 1769. The measurements were not to the required precision, not helped by hot, windy weather conditions, but the viewing was still considered a success.

From Taylor Road on the south side of the highway you can cycle 28km along a fire trail to The Oaks Picnic Ground in the National Park at Glenbrook. Children going for a short walk from Blaxland have found this trail and ended up in Woodford by mistake!

Hazelbrook – Jewel of the Mountains

Selwood Science and Puzzles, just across from the Railway Station, has a room of puzzles for you to try. Puzzles, science kits, and science books for sale, or if you don't want to be baffled they also serve tea and coffee. If approaching from the west use the U-turn bay just past the Hazelbrook bridge. 'Selwood' is a classic mid-Victorian house classified by the National Trust.

From the antique shops head down Terrace Falls Road for the walk to Victor Falls and Terrace Falls, one of the area's most picturesque walks, particularly after a drop of rain when at Terrace Falls the creek cascades over several ledges in a series of waterfalls. You can return via Bath Road, past the dilapidated Hazelbrook Swimming Pool (made by damming a swamp) or walk to Honour Avenue, Lawson from Bedford Creek.

The main walk in North Hazelbrook goes between Winbourne Road (turn right at the traffic lights) and Oaklands Road, and takes in a number of waterfalls and gives views of the amphitheatre. The start of the walk is beside 122 Winbourne Road.

Katoomba Falls.

Between Hazelbrook and Lawson turn right into Queen Street and then into Kangaroo Street to see a carving of a kangaroo. Photos are best taken in morning and afternoon shadows. The road sign on entering Lawson tells us this is 'The Original Blue Mountain'. Which isn't wrong. Following Queens Road into Binnowee Drive the 727 metre high 'Blue Mountain' is on the right, It is thought that the mid-Mountains were used by Aborigines as religious and ceremonial sites rather than for year-round living.

The North Lawson Park walk starts at the bottom of San Jose Avenue and goes to Dante's Glen, Empire Pass and Frederica Falls. A common tree in the rainforest areas here is coachwood (*Ceratopetalum apetalum*), recognised by the pink or green lichen which covers its bark. The walk finishes at Hugh Street and takes about four hours.

The village of Bullaburra just past Lawson is an Aboriginal word meaning 'blue sky' or 'fine weather'. Bullaburra is known to locals as the place where the mist starts (or stops).

Wentworth Falls

Kings Tableland to the left off the highway is named after an 883 metre high hill called Kings Table on the east side of Tablelands Road. There is an Aboriginal cave shelter and axe grinding grooves nearby (turn left off Kings Tableland Road into Queen Elizabeth Drive). Kings Tableland Observatory at 55 Hordern Road is open to the public on Friday, Saturday and Sunday evenings from 7pm (from 8pm during daylight saving).

Wentworth Falls Lake was made to store water for steam engines and is now a pleasant picnic spot and park. Turn right off the highway onto Station Street; drive past the shops and over the railway bridge, then turn left through a beautiful maple avenue. If you continue on past the Lake you will come back to the highway. Turn left and then right for the back route to Leura or turn right for Leura Mall and Katoomba.

James Blackhouse, a Quaker missionary, travelled across the Mountains in 1835. In the Wentworth Falls area he described the 'Blue Mountain Parrot, partly blue, and with a breast of crimson as brilliant as the flowers' and wrote that a:

> brown Honey-eater was darting its tongue, like a slender pencil of hair, into the elegant pink flowers of Grevillea linearis. Gompholobium grandiflorium, a large yellow, pea-flowered shrub of great beauty…enlivened the solitude and beguiled the walk of thirty-one miles through this dreary forest, which we accomplished in ten hours.

The Conservation Hut in Fletcher Street has a café and is an information centre for local walks (they sell booklets, and have a good map outside). The Valley of the Waters walk starts here, and connects with the National Pass, Overcliff and Wentworth Pass walks which lead to the picnic area at the end of Falls Road. The Nature Walk also starts here and goes along the Valley of the Waters creek. Princes Rock Lookout and several other walks start from the end of Falls Road picnic area, where there is another good map, and often an ice cream van. These are dramatic walks with great views over the Jamison Valley, but beware, most have steep sections. Falls Road and the Conservation Hut are also linked by

The old casino at the Hydro Majestic Hotel.

Left page: Federal Pass.

The Gatekeeper's Cottage, Medlow Bath.

A glimpse of the Grose Valley through the gum trees on the Pulpit Rock Track.

Bridal Veil Falls near Govett's Leap.

Previous pages: Early morning mist in the Grose Valley, photographed from Govett's Leap.

the Short Cut Walk (30minutes), which goes through bush behind the houses.

If coming for a short stay to the Mountains, and you enjoy walking, there are three walks I'd recommend not to miss. The first, for which you should allow five hours, is from the picnic area at the end of Falls Road, along the National Pass to the Valley of the Waters, then returning to Falls Road by the Overcliff and Undercliff Walk. The walk starts with a breathtaking section chiselled out of the cliff above Wentworth Falls, then follows National Pass, which isn't down in the valley but follows a ledge halfway up the escarpment with views of the Jamison Valley. National Pass leads into the Valley of the Waters which must surely be the most beautiful place in the whole of the Blue Mountains, a series of waterfalls cascading through a steep valley surrounded by rainforest, mossy rocks and ferns. On the way back to the picnic area the Undercliff Walk is another exciting section, following a ledge just below the cliff-top. The other 'don't miss' walks are at Katoomba and Blackheath.

Leura – The garden village

Leura Mall has a number of art and craft shops and fine restaurants and coffee shops. If your children have been behaving well they are permitted to visit the Candy Store in the arcade which has an enormous range of sweets.

Leura is well known for its exotic gardens. Everglades is open throughout the year and others are open during the Garden Festival in October. Everglades and a number of other gardens were designed by Paul Sorenson, the Danish landscape gardener after whom a bridge over the highway is named.

Leuralla, a large family home built just before World War 1, now houses a Toy and Railway Museum and a Memorial Museum to Dr HV Evatt, who must be important because he is seen photographed with General Macarthur, Sir Robert Menzies and the Queen Mother. Toys on display include zoo settings, a Noddy car, 'The genuine Princess Elizabeth' doll, cabinets full of Barbie dolls, including one in a wheelchair, and the Millennium Princess Barbie. For the rail enthusiast there is a collection of railway memorabilia and models in the garden.

There are lookouts and pleasant relatively flat walks at Leura. From Gordon Falls Reserve turn right for the Prince Henry Cliff Walk, and left for Lyrebird Dell and the Pool of Siloam. For the masochist from Leura Falls Picnic Area on Cliff Drive Dardanells Pass and Federal Pass drop down into the valley for a trek to the base of the Giant Stairway at the Three Sisters and on to the base of the Scenic Railway.

Katoomba – Home of Yulefest

Accommodation bookings and information are available at Wonderland Information Centre, 157 Lurline Street, just near the Three Sisters.

Mountainlink buses run seven days a week from Katoomba Station to Echo Point, the Three Sisters, Leura, and Blackheath. Pearce's bus company has a trolley bus service (a bus that looks like an old trolley bus) that meets each train, and there is an Explorer bus that leaves from Katoomba station and takes in many tourist sites. Mountain Top Trike Tours, based at the Scenic Skyway, offers motorbike joy rides and day tours.

One of the local landmarks is the Carrington Hotel on Katoomba Street, established in 1880. The hotel was renamed after Lord Carrington, with his permission, after he stayed there. A power station was built in 1911 to supply the hotel and the growing town with electricity. The chimney is a useful reference point for bushwalkers. The Clarendon guesthouse offers accommodation and interesting entertainment (music and cabaret shows). The popular YHA Hostel nearby outgrew its old premises and has just moved to the old Bible College building in Katoomba Street.

There is a variety of restaurants and cafés. Bushwalkers head to Aroney's milkbar for thick, smooth hot chocolates. The Paragon Café, famous for its chocolates, is classified by the National Trust. Aboriginal Dreamtime in Lurline Street sells art and craft and serves Aboriginal meats such as kangaroo, emu and crocodile. From June to August places from Wentworth Falls to Jenolan Caves host Yulefest celebrations to allow people the fun of a winter Christmas.

The Edge cinema screens large-screen movies (similar to IMAX). To get there turn right at the Council traffic lights. One of the movies shows a helicopter trip to see the recently-discovered Wollemi Pine, a tree dating to the time of the dinosaurs found in the wilderness of Wollemi National Park to the north.

Katoomba offers tourists adventure holidays including abseiling, canyoning, bushwalking, corporate training and women's empowerment (this is serious fun)!

The ten-minute walk from Echo Point to the Three Sisters is the most popular walk in the Mountains. Echo Point is also the most popular lookout for bus tours coming up for the day from Sydney. The first sister is connected to the main plateau by a small bridge. The Three Sisters and Katoomba Falls Reserve are floodlit from dusk until 11pm. The lights attract moths, and the moths attract bats which live in small caves under the lookout. In Aboriginal legend, the Three Sisters, Menhi, Weemalah and Gunnedoo were turned to stone by their father, who was killed before he could turn them back. Twenty cents in the slot at the sculpture fountain at the Scenic Skyway tells the story in more detail.

The Scenic Skyway cable car five minutes west of Echo Point by car on Cliff Drive takes you for a five-minute ride above the valley floor. From the cable car there are great views of the Three Sisters, Katoomba Falls and Orphan Rock.

The Scenic Railway takes tourists down and up the mountain on a railway line originally used for hauling coal. In 1933 tourists travelled in a coal truck, and later a twelve-seater carriage called 'The Mountain Devil' was used. This is the world's steepest incline railway with a maximum grade of 52 degrees. The ride is pretty thrilling, as the screams you hear suggest. If you are trying to hold a backpack, or, worse still, a child, it is even more terrifying. The view, however, is terrific, and people vie for the front seat.

A good way to see the area is to walk down the Furber Steps which begin at the rear of the Scenic Railway Complex. This is the second of the 'don't miss' walks in the Mountains. There are about 1000 steps to the lower platform of the Scenic Railway, where you can catch the train for the uphill journey. On the way down there are two side paths to different levels of Katoomba Falls. Beyond the station you can see the old coal mine entrances one of which has an audiovisual display inside. Pit ponies used to pull skips of coal along this path. If you continue on this walk it's about a five hour return trip across the landslide, to a rock formation called the Ruined Castle which has a panoramic view of the surroundings

Lush ferns often line tracks on the sheltered lower slopes.

A section of the Grand Canyon Track.

Hanging Rock in the Grose Valley is accessed by a dirt road outside Blackheath.

The road leading to Hanging Rock.

A favourite location for landscape artists, the Grose Valley close to Hanging Rock.

Like a peeling banana; a tree shedding its skin on the Fairy Bower Track, Mount Victoria.

and makes an excellent location to stop for a picnic lunch.

Shale mining started in the Ruined Castle area in 1889. Miners used to live here, but when the mine closed the tents and houses were pulled down and the materials taken back to Katoomba. Traces of one or two of the miner's stone dwellings can be seen next to the track. The Golden Stairs (named after a song the Salvation Army sang on the way down them) provided access for miners from the Ruined Castle mining village to Katoomba, and now offers walkers an alternative route for the return trip.

If you go east from the Scenic Railway platform you pass a 500-year old turpentine tree and get to the base of Katoomba Falls. From here the track continues through a lush forest to the Giant Stairway (keep the kids going by asking them to count the steps), the Three Sisters and Echo Point. Allow three hours for this walk including the return trip to the Scenic Railway by Prince Henry Cliffwalk.

Medlow Bath

Medlow Bath is dominated by the Hydro Majestic Hotel (built 1880 to 1903). From the rooms and the hotel café there's a spectacular view over the valley. This building was once home to the retailer Mark Foy, who built many of the tracks in the area. For a while it was a Hydropathic Sanatorium offering mud baths, cleansing regimes and cures such as Bowel Kneading and Centrifugal Douching (whatever that was). Just past the Hydro Majestic you can see one of the early gatehouses (1867) built where the railway crossed the road before the bridge was built.

The Medlow Bath Old Post Office bookshop on the north side of the station sells second hand books and light snacks including goulash and Devonshire teas.

Blackheath – Rhododendron town

Blackheath is a pleasant town, and has retained a lot of its historic character. Early on, though, Henry Anthill, who travelled with Governor Macquarie in 1815, wrote: 'From the appearance of this station, it being a kind of a heath, but a very wild and dreary scenery, the Governor gave it the name of Blackheath, though to my eye, very unlike its namesake'.

On your left as you approach the traffic lights is a park with a sculpture of a man on horseback. This commemorates the incorrect myth that Govett's Leap was named after a bushranger who jumped off the cliff rather than be caught by his pursuers. The truth is somewhat more mundane – the falls were named after the surveyor William Romaine Govett, who discovered them in 1832.

A splash of colour in the Australian bush – Bacchante Gardens Blackheath.

Blackheath Rhododendron Festival is held every year in the first week of November. Many varieties of rhododendrons can be seen in flower from late October to early November in Blackheath Memorial Garden, signposted off Govett's Leap Road. In a less formal bush setting Bacchante Gardens (follow the signs off the highway at Sturt Street) has beautiful beds of azaleas, rhododendrons and Australian native flowers. At Bacchante Gardens, which open all year, biscuits and coffee are sold by volunteers from mid-October to mid-November.

The main attraction of Blackheath is the stunning views and stimulating walks into the Grose Valley, including one to the Blue Gum Forest next to the creek on the valley floor. This walk is a tough one-day slog or a more comfortable two days if you camp in the forest. The National Park Centre at the end of Govett's Leap Road (turn right at the traffic lights off the highway) can advise on walks and camping, and alternative activities for misty weather. When you walk carry drinking water and warm, waterproof clothes. Take your time and enjoy your walks. As Jim Smith says, 'With years of experience you can learn to make a half-kilometre walk last all day.'

The National Parks Centre also has displays and video presentations, and sells walking guides, maps and nature-based gifts. It also runs guided walks and activities throughout the Mountains, especially during school holidays. Behind the Centre is the 1.8km Fairfax Heritage Track, which gives an easy introduction to the plant communities of the area, including hanging swamps and heath. Spotted pardalotes, grey shrike thrushes and grey currawongs are regular visitors. The path can be used by people in wheelchairs and by prams.

Govett's Leap lookout just down the hill from the National Park Centre is the most spectacular anywhere in the Blue Mountains. From Govett's Leap it's a ninety minute walk to Evan's Lookout, named after the surveyor. On the way, 20 minutes out from Govett's Leap, the track crosses the creek above Bridal Veil Falls. An alternative route to Evans Lookout is by the Evans Lookout Road on the right before you come into Blackheath. This is also the way to get to the last but certainly not least of the three Blue Mountains 'must see' walks. It's a round trip of five kilometres that can be done comfortably in four hours. The starting point is Neate's Glen, signposted on the right side of the Evans Lookout Road. The track drops down through clumps of tree ferns into the little lost world of the Grand Canyon, a steep-sided gorge with ferns and rainforest trees clinging to the rocks on either side of a little creek. The track winds back up out of the canyon to Evans Lookout, from where it's 20 minutes walk back along Evans Lookout Road to return to the car.

Some of the many shades of rhododendrons that bloom in the Mountains in spring.

Megalong Valley

Aborigines and white settlers lived in harmony in the Megalong Valley, even fielding two cricket teams. Gundungara people had always passed this way between their winters in Burragorang and summers in Wallerawang. The same route was later used by stockmen.

To reach the valley turn left off the Highway at the Blackheath traffic lights over the level crossing, then immediately left, right, then left at the big Megalong sign. The Megalong Valley is a rural part of the Mountains. Horseriding is available, and the Australian Heritage Centre presents Aboriginal corroborees and sheep-shearing demonstrations. Pull off on the left as you go down into the valley to see the creek, rainforest and tree ferns on the Coachwood Glen nature track.

Mount Victoria

Early roads cost a lot to maintain and the Government paid for their upkeep by charging tolls. Turnpike gates and a stone cottage for the gatekeeper were erected at Mount Victoria in 1849, and can be seen on your left as you enter the town. You can also park here for Fairy Bower walks. The Government set the tolls, but earned its money by selling the rights to collect them (an early taste of privatisation).

Mount Victoria was a busy railway station, and its scale is a reminder of its importance. The Mount Victoria Museum is housed in part of the old Railway Refreshment Rooms which closed in 1960. Upstairs were bedrooms for passengers who had to wait for horsedrawn transport to pick them up. The Museum is open from 2pm to 5pm each Saturday, Sunday, Public Holiday and school holidays. It features Kate Kelly's bed (sister of Ned) and various old gadgets including a Victor marmalade slicer, a knife cleaner (pre-stainless steel) and an Ezy beat water driven mixer. They also have on display a 'Mystery object', asking whether any visitors can identify it. (The consensus is that it is a tool for stretching things – perhaps straw for hats, or raffia, or leather.)

The strange sight of a Tyrolean manor house in the Australian bush. Caves House Jenolan Caves.

Nearby Mount Vic Flicks is a terrific old-style movie theatre with showings Thursday to Sunday in the Mount Victoria Public Hall (built 1934).

Mount York

Turn right onto Mount York Road from the Great Western Highway about a kilometre after Mount Victoria, the starting point for several walks on early disused roads which descended the mountain. First you come to Lawson's Long Alley, built from 1822 to 1823, where a short walk takes you to a drainage culvert and handpicked drains cut by convicts. In spring there are lots of egg-and-bacon pea flower, and purple creeping *Hardenbergia*. Across the road Berghofer's Pass built by a German immigrant has views over the valley. It was an alternative road for early motor vehicles that lacked the power to get up Victoria Pass. The name of the pass chiselled into a rock above the road was defaced during the First World War.

Drive to the end of the Mount York Road, where a plethora of monuments commemorate the early explorers. In 1900 an obelisk was built by public subscription to commemorate the first three explorers, as well as Evans the surveyor, Cox the road-builder, and Macquarie the planner. Look out to Mount Blaxland, the furthest point the explorers reached.

Cox's Road the first road down Mount York was used by Macquarie in 1815 when he made the first journey by carriage across the Mountains. Pick marks show where the road had to be widened to allow his vehicle through. Lockyer's Road, with wide bends and an even grade, was built from 1828 to 1829, but construction stopped when Mitchell transferred the road gangs to work on his own project down Victoria Pass. Traffic on the Great Western Highway still thunders across the convict-built sandstone embankment of Victoria Pass on the descent of the mountain just outside Mount Victoria.

A writer using the initials X.Y.Z. wrote to the *Australian* newspaper about the descent of Mount York:

> We soon arrived at the bottom, where the ground was strewn with fallen trees, in great numbers, all regularly arranged by the roadside. As the country was by no means thinly timbered, I could not conceive what these trees were intended for…It appears that all carts coming down the Big Hill as this is called, must, ere they descend, cut down a tree at the top, to fix behind the dray, instead of locking the wheel. … We were now in the Vale of Clwydd…and after a smart ride of two miles, along the valley, we arrived at Collett's [sic] Inn, the Golden Fleece, the 'rest and be thankful' of the Blue Mountains.

Collit's Inn still stands in Hartley Vale, now a private house painted aqua and yellow. The Comet Inn built in 1879, and named after the brand of kerosene produced in the valley, is nearby. The Lockyer's Track and Lawson's Long Alley historic walks end at Hartley Vale.

Hartley Historic Site

Hartley Historic Site is on the left of the Great Western Highway just before the Jenolan Caves turnoff. Business in Hartley stagnated when the railway was built through Lithgow in 1869, and the town has been preserved very much in its original 1800s state. Seventeen buildings remain, and some are leased to individuals. A lovely place to live, if you don't mind being a tourist attraction.

You can tour the Courthouse for $4 per adult if there are enough people. It was designed by the colonial architect Mortimer Lewis and was built in 1837 from pit-sawn timber and hand-forged nails. Crimes and punishments are recorded in the Hartley Bench Book Records. In 1838, for example, Thomas Kenny had 25 lashes for neglect of duty in losing sheep and Maria Osborne was in solitary confinement on bread and water for three days for being drunk and disorderly. Prisoners in the cells carved their initials, stylised Norfolk Island Pines (Norfolk Island penal colony was considered 'hell on earth') and the name of the unpopular 'TS Miller, The Hangman, Dog informer'.

Jenolan Caves

Jenolan Caves can be reached in an hour via Hampton. The caves were known to the local Aborigines as 'Benomera', meaning holes in a hill, which seems like a pretty good description. Tourists used to come by train to Tarana station where they changed to a horse and buggy for the rough dirt road to the caves. This trip took 24 hours. In 1886 a bridle track was completed from Katoomba through the Megalong (then Kanimbla) Valley and up the Black Range to Jenolan Caves. In 1984 the Lands Department reopened the 'Six Foot Track' for use by bushwalkers, who usually take three days to complete the 45km trek. There are four campgrounds along the trail, and guided tours are also available. If

St Bernard's Catholic Church (1848) from the Presbytery (1850s) at Hartley.

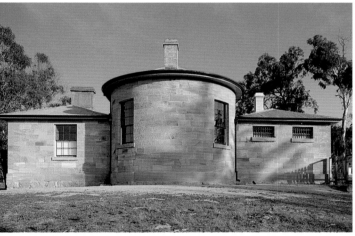

Hartley Courthouse.

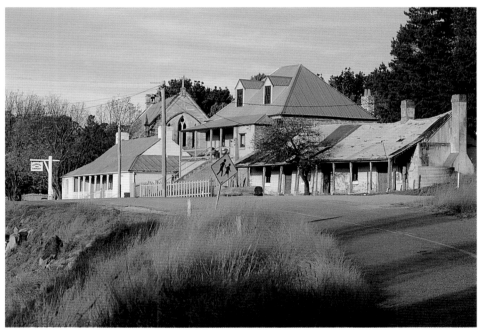

Hartley village.

Autumn colours at Mt Wilson.

The Zig-Zag railway, now a tourist attraction, uses the original route that descended the Blue Mountains at Clarence.

you start at Jenolan Caves you end up at Nellies Glen, near the Explorer's Tree, Katoomba.

Grand Arch offers a dramatic entrance to Jenolan Caves, as you drive through an open-ended cave. Accommodation is available at Caves House, a three-storey guesthouse that has been open to visitors since 1906. You can tour nine show caves, and also adventure caves where you wear a light on your helmet and clamber over undeveloped rock. There are picnic facilities here and beautiful walks. Wombats and rock wallabies live in the area.

Oberon and Kanangra–Boyd National Park

Oberon is situated amongst forest plantations, and is a good place for fossicking, fishing and mushroom picking.

The Kanangra–Boyd National Park can be reached from Jenolan Caves or Oberon over a rough road. Kanangra Walls lookout has great views across Grand Gorge and is the start of three short walks. Longer walks offer opportunities for solitude for experienced bushwalkers.

From Jenolan Caves or Oberon return to the plateau of the Mountains the way you came, or through Lithgow. The Darling Causeway connects the ridges to the north and south of the Grose River, and carries the road and railway between Mount Victoria and Bell.

Tree ferns flourish on the rich basalt soils of Mt Wilson.

Clarence and the Zig-Zag railway

The Great Zig-Zag Railway was built in 1869 in the form of a 'Z' to take the train down to the Lithgow Valley. The train goes along the 'zig', changes the engine to the other end, goes down the 'zag' in the middle, then swaps the engine again to make the return journey on the way up. The line passes through two tunnels and over three sandstone viaducts, built from locally quarried sandstone. The viaducts are stronger now than they were when they were built, as the vibration of the trains has compacted the mortarless stones tighter together. Bottlenecks developed when train numbers increased, so in 1910 a double line deviation through the escarpment was opened, and the Zig-Zag closed. The viaducts and cuttings remained a curiosity for passing bushwalkers until the Zig-Zag reopened as a tourist attraction in the 1980s.

Access to the Zig-Zag Railway is at Clarence between Lithgow and Bell. If travelling up from Sydney by train let the guard know you wish to stop at the Zig-Zag Railway and the train will make a special stop to let you off near the Zig-Zag Railway's Bottom Points Station. You can travel up and down the hill at the Zig-Zag on foot, by rail motor (diesel), and, on weekends and during school holidays by steam train. Steam locomotives can be inspected in the workshops close to Bottom Points Station.

Mount Wilson

Heading back towards Sydney on Bell's Line of Road the turnoff for Mount Wilson is 10 kilometres past the junction of Darling Causeway. As the road winds up towards Mt Wilson you will notice a sudden change from open sclerophyll forest to dense, ferny rainforest supported by the rich soil of the basalt-capped mountain.

Mount Wilson has cool-climate exotic plants in street avenues and in private gardens open for public viewing. Some are open all year, others in spring and autumn, and some just on weekends. Entry is not cheap, but the gardens are substantial. One of the best known properties, Nooroo, meaning 'shady place', was built in 1880 by William Hay from local pit-sawn timber. The garden contains a pink horse chestnut grown from seed from Wynstay (another old property in Mount Wilson), and a white crab apple raised from seed from College Gardens, Cambridge. The old tennis court is now a formal garden with clematis and wisteria, worth a special journey to see when it's in bloom in spring.

There are many pleasant walks around Mount Wilson. Brochures are available in the Old Post Office Café. A short but interesting one is the Cathedral of Ferns walk, on the way out of Mt Wilson towards Mt Irvine which starts across the road from the picnic spot and takes about ten minutes. For the more adventurous, a walk starts close by into the valley of the Wollangambe River. Take a li-lo with you and float down the river.

Mount Tomah

On the way to Mount Tomah you pass Pierce's Pass Picnic Area on the right. Pierce's Pass is the easiest way into the Grose Valley, built in about 1930 by Bert Pierce and Clarrie Hungerford to take cattle to the flats near the Blue Gum Forest. Descendants of the Hungerford family co-wrote the book *Exploring the Blue Mountains*, and another family

Scenery in Mt Wilson.

The Avenue, Mt Wilson.

The Cathedral of Ferns, Mt Wilson.

member, Hesba Brinsmead, wrote children's books set in the area.

Mount Tomah Botanic Garden is on the right of the highway. It was established by the Sydney Botanic Gardens for the growth of cool-climate plants, on the site of a flower farm. The 'Explorer's Walk' is one of many beautiful walks in the Garden. It winds through beds of bushes and flowers from the Himalaya, India, Burma, China and South East Asia. Notices on the way document the European discovery of these plants in the nineteenth century and the sometimes clandestine methods used to bring plants and seedlings back to Europe. Twelve Wollemi pines have been planted on the Gondwana walk. They were discovered only in 1994 and come from an evolutionary line thought to be extinct. Their bark looks like 'bubbling chocolate' and they are bisexual, with both male and female reproductive cones on the same tree. What's the world coming to.

Bilpin and Kurrajong Heights

Bilpin is famous for its apple orchards developed after the Second World War. Street-side stalls sell juice, fruit and vegetables, including tree-ripened, wax-free fruit. At Bilpin Fruit Bowl visitors are welcome to use the barbecue hot plates in the picnic area.

Kurrajong means 'shade tree', and in early days the seeds of this tree were roasted as a coffee substitute. Kurrajong Heights offers Grass Karts for the adventurer and an Opal Shop and Museum for the shopper. Lochiel House, built about 1825, is the oldest building in Kurrajong Heights. For many years it was a guesthouse known as Ivy Lodge; it now houses the Lochiel Café.

At Kurrajong the road drops down the escarpment to the Hawkesbury River valley and the way back to Sydney is through Richmond and Windsor. You have finished your tour of the City of the Blue Mountains, the City within a National Park.

One of the best times to visit Mt Tomah is in spring, when plants such as this pink ice protea are in bloom.

Mt Tomah is the cool climate garden of the Royal Botanic Gardens.

Sydney's Southern Beaches

Bondi Beach and the southern beaches.

Sydney's Southern Beaches

If Captain (then Lieutenant) Cook noticed Sydney's Southern Beaches on leaving Botany Bay in 1770 he made no mention of them in his diary, but did note 'a Bay or Harbour where there appeared to be safe anchorage which I called Port Jackson.' When Governor Phillip sailed past on his way to explore Port Jackson (Sydney Harbour) 18 years later, no one in his entourage mentioned the beaches either, though the Judge Advocate, David Collins, who was on the expedition, wrote that as they made their way up the coast their boats

> Attracted the attention of several parties of the natives … who all greeted them in the same words, and in the same tone of vociferation, shouting everywhere 'Warra, Warra, Warra' – words which, by the gestures that accompanied them, could not be interpreted into invitations to land, or expressions of welcome.

In fact the Aborigines were telling the First Fleeters to 'go away.' But Phillip took no notice and after rounding South Head landed at a little bay which has ever since been known as 'Camp Cove.' It was the first place where Europeans stepped ashore in Sydney Harbour.

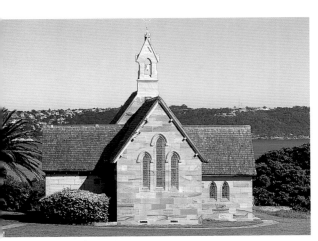

St Peter's Church, Watsons Bay.

Robertson Park, Watsons Bay.

Watsons Bay

Camp Cove is in Watsons Bay, named after Robert Watson, Quartermaster of the *Sirius*, the flagship of the First Fleet.

After being posted to the Signal Station in 1791, then working as Harbour Master controlling the pilot boats at Watsons Bay, Watson was made the first lighthouse keeper when the Macquarie Lighthouse started operations in 1816 and maintained the light until he died in 1819.

Watsons Bay is still the base for pilot boats operating in the harbour. In the early days pilots lived in huts on Camp Cove and worked for themselves with their own boats and crews who were often ex-whalers. A competitive system existed and the first crew to reach a vessel entering Sydney piloted it down the harbour. Sometimes boats would row as far south as Jervis Bay on the lookout for a ship. On 20th July 1867 a pilot boat rowed out in a southerly gale to meet the full-rigged sailing ship the *Strathdon* off the heads. The pilot boat capsized and two other boats while attempting to rescue the stricken crew. In all seven men were drowned and not long after the Government stopped the competitive pilot system and pressed into service the first steam pilot boat the *Thetis*. These days the modern orange and blue pilot boats moor at the pilot station at Watsons Bay next to the harbourside baths at Gibsons Beach.

Close by where Old South Head Road terminates near the water, is an old obelisk, which reads 'This road made By Subscription was compleated in Ten Weeks from the 25 of March 1811 By 21 soldiers of His Majesty 73 Reghtment'. Perhaps it was chiselled by an uneducated convict forger.

The first South Head Road started at the southeast corner of Hyde Park, the site of Sydney's racecourse in the early days of the colony, and finished at Watsons Bay eight miles away. Paid for by voluntary subscription and completed in ten weeks, the road was 'well covered with gravel of good quality.' The section between Hyde Park and Bondi Junction was later renamed Oxford Street. According to the *Sydney Gazette* of 15th January 1820 'an excursion to South Head… [was] one of the most agreeable rides that imagination could contemplate.'

Further along the bay is the ferry wharf, from where a service runs to Circular Quay on weekends, public holidays and at lunchtime on weekdays. At lunch or suppertime many of the passengers are bound for nearby Doyle's Restaurant on the beachfront at Watsons Bay. It is Australia's most famous seafood restaurant and has been owned and operated by the same family for over 100 years. There's something quite magical about sitting at an outside table at Doyle's on a summer's evening watching the city lights come on in Sydney nine kilometres away across the harbour.

South Head

Walk along Cliff Street to Camp Cove and up the wooden steps at the north end of the

The harbour-front at Watsons Bay with Dunbar House in the background.

Doyle's Restaurant at Watsons Bay has been run by the same family for over 100 years.

Lady Bay nudist beach, on the walk from Camp Cove to South Head.

131

Hornby Lighthouse, South Head.

beach, which is the starting point for a 40 minute return walk to South Head. The cobbled stone roadway just above the steps was used to transport ordnance from a military wharf on Camp Cove to the guns of South Head Battery. As the cliff-edge track leads above the water to the head it passes fortifications dating from the 1870s to the Second World War. On the way, you pass Lady Bay beach, which for many years had been an unofficial nudist beach where in 1975 it was raided by the police who arrested 35 men and women for 'indecent exposure.' After an appeal by a man against his conviction was upheld in a Court of Criminal Appeal a cabinet subcommittee was set up to look into the matter which after due consideration made Lady Bay an 'official' nude bathing beach.

At the tip of the headland stands the red and white striped Hornby Lighthouse erected in 1858 following the tragic shipwreck of the migrant ship *Dunbar* at The Gap in 1857. The lighthouse was named in honour of Lady Denison, wife of the then Governor. She was the daughter of Admiral Sir Phipps Hornby. A ship which has the lighthouse on its port beam is considered to have entered the harbour.

The Gap

Returning to Watsons Bay, a path above Military Road opposite Robertson Park leads to the cliff-top lookout at The Gap. Sydney's worst ever tragedy took place at The Gap on the night of 20th August 1857 when the migrant ship *Dunbar* was blown onto the rocks in a southerly gale. No one was aware the ship had foundered and it wasn't until the following morning that the wreckage was sighted. Out of the 122 on board only one man, Able Seaman James Johnson survived by clinging to a rock ledge where he was spotted 36 hours after the ship went down. Johnson was later appointed lighthouse keeper at Nobbys Head at the entrance to Newcastle Harbour. The anchor of the *Dunbar*, recovered in 1907, is set in concrete at the edge of the cliff.

Possibly because of the association of Watsons Bay with tragedy, the cliffs at The Gap became Sydney's traditional location for suicides. The tram terminus was near the cliff-top, within spitting distance of the cliff edge, and conductors were warned to look out for melancholy or distracted passengers. Sometimes the long tram ride out from the city gave would-be suicides time to change their minds, and on more than one occasion a conductor was able to talk a lost soul out of a drastic course of action.

Near the road the tiny St Peter's Church of England designed by Edmund Blacket and completed in 1864, was built on the hill so it would be the first building to greet the eyes of passengers arriving in Sydney by ship. The organ in the church, built by Robert and William Grey of London in 1796, was lent to Napoleon when he was in exile on St Helena. After being returned to England and installed in a Somerset rural church the organ was brought out to Sydney where it was used to teach music at the Conservatorium of Music. The organ was installed at St Peters as a memorial to the fallen servicemen of the district in the First World War.

The Signal Station

Just below the Dunbar Memorial Lookout a track leads south along the old tram cutting, then through The Gap Park to the Signal Station on Old South Head Road. On the return journey through The Gap Park make sure to take the alternative route back to Military Road down 'Jacob's Ladder.' The path follows a gully through a long extinct volcanic dyke sheltered by the spreading branches and tree ferns of a pocket of rainforest.

The Signal Station was established originally in January 1790, when Governor Phillip, anxious that the expected Second Fleet may miss the opening of Sydney Harbour, sent a party of men to the head to erect a signal flagstaff and keep a fire burning at night. As David Collins noted:

> To this point were the walks of the inhabitants of Port Jackson daily directed, fondly indulging a pleasing delusion that the very circumstance of looking for a sail would bring one into view.

The present hexagonal stone building was designed by colonial architect Mortimer Lewis and erected by convict labour in 1840. The station has been

The rugged cliffs of South Head protect Sydney Harbour from ocean swells.

The Gap, Watsons Bay.

Camp Cove was the first place where Europeans stepped ashore in Sydney Harbour.

The view of Sydney Harbour from South Head.

Macquarie Lighthouse.

When Charles Darwin arrived in Sydney by ship he thought the deserted yellow cliffs looked more like the coast of Patagonia than the outskirts of a busy city.

As clean as bright white sheets hanging on the line. Even in the day Macquarie Lighthouse looks like a white beacon shining out to sea.

continuously manned since 1790 and shipping movements are logged from the tower to this day.

Following the cliff-top track behind the Signal Station for a further five minutes brings you to the majestic tall brilliantly white painted Macquarie Lighthouse. The original lighthouse on the site, Australia's first, was designed by the convict architect Francis Greenway. The present structure, very similar in design to the original, was built in 1883 after the sandstone of Greenway's lighthouse decayed in the salt air.

Waverley

From Watsons Bay it's a five-minute drive to Bondi. Continue south on Old South Head and drive straight on at the roundabout next to South Head Cemetery. 'Welcome to the Municipality of Waverley, A Nuclear Free Zone' reads a sign by the road. The council district of Waverley, which includes Bondi, Tamarama and Bronte beaches within its boundary, was named after a house which once stood on Old South Head Road. It was built by Barnett Levey, who arrived in Sydney on the convict transport the *John Bull* on 18th December 1821 with about 20 other free settlers and 80 female convicts. Barnett had come to Sydney to join his brother Solomon Levey, who ran his various business interests from a building at 72 George Street where Dymock's Arcade now stands.

In 1829 Barnett Levey built Sydney's first theatre at the rear of 72 George Street financed through a share-offering, though the cost of the project meant he had to give up his own interest to the other share-holders shortly after it opened. On the eve of the day on which he was to transfer ownership Barnett Levey appeared on stage and sang 'My Love is Gone to Botany Bay.'

Perhaps he was strapped for cash because at that time Levey had already embarked on construction of a house in the present vicinity of Hollywood Avenue, the *Sydney Gazette* reporting in November 1827

> This splendid building ... [which] has a commanding view of Sydney to the west and of the ocean to the east, has been named by the proprietor 'Waverley House' in honour of Sir Walter Scott.

Scott was the author of 'Waverley Novels' a series of romances on Scottish history. They included 'Waverley' published in 1814, the name of the title apparently deriving from the Abbey of the Blessed Mary of Waverley, near Farnham in Surrey, England.

Waverley House was completed in 1829, and offered for let, but Barnett Levey was dispossessed the following year, the property sold on 4th February 1830 by the Sheriff to cover a debt to John Morison, McDonald and Campbell. Waverley House, which became known as 'Levey's Folly' was taken over by the Catholic Church and used as an orphanage for destitute children. During the time he owned the property, which covered 60 acres, Levey laid out a street plan using names from other Scott novels. Some of these survive, including Woodstock and Kenilworth Streets at Bondi Junction.

Bondi Beach

To continue to Bondi, turn left on Military Road just past Diamond Bay Bowling Club and follow it as it winds through the suburb of Rose Bay North. Anyone who has run or walked in the annual City to Surf fun-run will be familiar with this route. Along the way it's worth stopping for five minutes at Dudley Page Reserve opposite Myuna Road in Dover Heights to admire the superb panorama of the city and harbour from the plateau. Returning to the car and continuing on Military Road there are tantalising glimpses through the houses from the heights of the Pacific, Bondi and the headlands of the southern beaches as far as Maroubra. Soon the road begins the gentle descent into Bondi, passing on the left, North Bondi golf links where there are some Aboriginal carvings on the cliff top.

Bondi needs no introduction. It's the most famous beach in Australia and along with Malibu, St Tropez and Brighton one of the most famous beaches in the world. But somehow it isn't quite what you expect. There's a beautiful crescent of white sand caressed by the white foam of Pacific breakers gently rolling in. But what about the rest. North Bondi is a toy town of three or four storey blocks of

Seagulls at Ben Buckler.

Seagulls at Bondi.

Shop-fronts on Bondi Road.

flats with names like 'Lurline' and 'Sunray.' On the beachfront there's another collection of three or four storey flats and guesthouses with titles like Majestic Mansions and The Empire. In between like a dividing line is the Bondi Beach Public School, its entrance shaded by a Doric columned portico. Step one or two streets back from the beachfront and there's a sense of decay and of glories lost. Bondi hasn't really changed since the 1920s when the seawall was completed. It's still a nice place though. And what child could ever take schoolwork seriously with Bondi Beach for a school playground.

Early history

Go back just another 40 years to 1880 and the beach was a lonely windswept stretch of sand backed by dunes with two houses in sight. Bondi Beach was private property.

In December 1809 the entire beach and 200 acres of the surroundings were granted to William Roberts

> his Heirs and Assigns, to have and to hold forever … Conditioned not to sell or alienate the same for the space of five years from the date hereof and to cultivate thirty acres within the said period … reserving for the use of the Crown such timbers may be fit for Naval purposes. Quit rent four shillings …

The boundaries of the grant were surveyed by the Irish convict surveyor James Meehan (who also cursed Dee Why for ever more with its name) the top of one of the pages in his field book reading 'Bundi Bay, Dec.11, 1809.' It was the first mention and spelling of the district which became known as Bondi, apparently after an Aboriginal word meaning 'water breaking over rocks.' Roberts didn't live at his farm at Bondi but in an inn he owned called the King's Arms on the corner of Hunter and Castlereagh Streets in Sydney. He obviously had some trouble with trespassers on his Bondi property because he placed a notice in the *Sydney Gazette* on 4th September 1819:

> Notice is hereby given that all persons are strictly forbidden to cut or carry away any Wood off Boondye on the South Head Road … Two Guineas reward.

Saturday morning at Bondi Beach.

The Bondi Estate stayed in the Roberts' family until 8th March 1851 when the entire 200 acres was sold for £200 to Edward Hall. After arriving in New South Wales as a free settler in 1811 Hall worked as a cashier in Australia's first bank, the Bank of New South Wales then founded one of the colony's first newspapers, the 'Sydney Monitor', in 1826. The estate passed to his editor, Francis O'Brien, who was married to Hall's daughter Georgina. O'Brien had previously been married to Hall's other daughter Sophia, but she'd died eighteen months after the wedding. Francis O'Brien lived in a house he built on the property 'Bondi Lodge.' Later re-named The Homestead, it was still standing until after the First World War.

Dawn sky from Bondi Pavilion.

The fact that this enormous beach, so close to Sydney, remained private property, concerned the government, the Surveyor General Sir Thomas Mitchell writing to Edward Hall on 29th September 1854

> I have learned that the public are wholly excluded from the beach at Bondi Bay, I have therefore to submit that access to this is indispensable … [and it] should be resumed, if necessary at the public expense, for the health and recreation of the inhabitants of Sydney.

Hall and O'Brien resisted all attempts by the government to resume or buy the beach, but they did allow access to part of the property as a public picnic ground and pleasure resort. Though even this permission Francis O'Brien threatened to withdraw, writing to Waverley Council in June 1877 because

> the grounds adjacent to the beach and homestead at Bondi, from the want of proper police supervision are becoming unfit, by reason of immoral practices for the purpose of recreation of families visiting the place; and I shall be compelled most unwillingly to withdraw the privilege of a permissive right to the public to use the grounds, which I have for so many years allowed, unless the same are placed under proper police supervision.

Efforts by the Council and Government were finally successful on 9th June 1882 when 25 acres at Bondi were resumed for public recreation, access to the beach was unrestricted for the first time and shortly after 'Bondi Park' at the beachfront was enclosed by a picket fence.

A Greek temple on Bondi beach-front.

Swimming at Bondi

Once the battle was won to allow unrestricted access to the beach, the next campaign was to secure unrestricted access for swimming. Bathing in the sea was prohibited under Section 77 of the Police Offences Act of 1901 between the hours of 8 a.m. and 8 p.m. People of course still bathed at the beach and after the Council received complaints that swimmers were dressed indecently the gentlemen of Waverley Council made an official beach inspection in 1907 and ruled that suitable attire was

> a guernsy with trouser legs, reaching from the elbow to the bend of the knee, together with a skirt attached to the front of the garment, apron fashion and covering the figure from hips to knees.

A demonstration took place at the beach against the ordnance, which was reported in the *Sydney Morning Herald* on 21st October 1907 under the headline 'Burlesque at Bondi.' The costume of one demonstrator

> was similar to the garb worn by the Roman centurions and was decidedly handsome, although like others in which the skirt was noticed, it was an effectual bar to good swimming and was indeed dangerous to wear in the water. Sairey Gamp with a poker bonnet and a gorgeous shawl was a prominent feature, but she had to be rescued when she tried to swim. One swimmer wore a doormat round his middle and was told he had no respect for the Mayor of Waverley (R. G. Watkins) as he was showing his bare toes ...

However the 'neck to knee' by-law remained and to ensure no one undressed in public bathing sheds for 750 men and 250 women were installed at the beach by the end of 1911.

As Bondi was the closest ocean beach to the city it was soon attracting large crowds. Bondi was the first beach to introduce car-parking charges in 1926, with a shilling per car for parking during a morning, afternoon or evening 'session.' The first accounting period showed an income of £353.15.0 for an expenditure of £86. Though before the Second World War most day-trippers to Bondi came by tram, which was extended to the beach in 1894. From Bondi Junction it ran down a long straight hill five kilometres long to Campbell Parade at the beach, frequently not stopping for passengers and giving rise to the expression 'shot through like a Bondi tram.'

Tamarama

From Notts Avenue at the south end of Bondi Beach a track leads after a twenty-minute walk over the cliffs to Tamarama. On the way you may notice a large boulder which sits on top of the rocks on the opposite headland of Bondi at Ben Buckler. According to a Council plaque fixed to the 235 ton rock it was washed there by a stupendous storm on 15th July 1912. A likely story if ever I heard one. Another story is that in the 1960s two gold mermaids graced the top of the rock. Though this one's true, they were placed there by the sculptor Lyall Randolph who was inspired by the Little Mermaid statue in Copenhagen. One was washed away by a storm in 1974 and the other, heavily weathered, now takes pride of place at the top of the stairs in Waverley Library.

Tamarama is a narrow beach; broader than it is long, backed by a grassy park nearly encircled by a high sandstone wall carrying Tamarama Marine Drive. If the wall extended across the narrow promenade it would be like Alcatraz prison yard. There's no escape. Overlooking it at the west end is a block of flats on the hill that must be the ugliest in Sydney. Even Alcatraz looks an architectural tour de force by comparison. On top of the beachfront café a State Bank clock with a square green face matches the green of the grass in the park.

Known in the past as 'Dixon's Bay' after a local landowner, 'Gamma Gamma' on old naval maps, 'Fletchers Glen' in the 1807s when David Fletcher the first Mayor of Waverley bought the beach and ten acres and built a home at the head of the gully, and now nick-named 'Glamourama', the view of Tamarama today looks tame compared to its appearance in photos taken 100 years ago. In 1887 'The Aquarium' opened on the heights above the north end of the beach which besides its namesake had a dancing hall, bowling alley, a skating rink and side shows including a shooting gallery. Over 5,000 people visited the complex on 2nd October 1887 its opening day. The depression of the 1890s saw the enterprise close in 1891 but it was expanded and re-opened in 1906 as 'Wonderland City' with a long big dipper running between the headlands across the top of the park and an 'aerial' boat like a flying gondola hanging by a wire strung between the cliffs above the beach. Though this enterprise too, closed not long after. When the land was sub-divided for housing the area on the north side was advertised as the 'Wonderland City Estate' and that on the south as 'Wonderland City Estate South.'

Bronte

Following the road above Tamarama takes you after another five minute walk to Bronte. Bronte Baths at the south end were the first public beach baths to be opened in Australia in 1887. According to the council regulations at the time they were

> to be opened for gentlemen from daylight to 10 a.m. and 4 p.m. till dark each day. The baths to be opened for ladies from 10 a.m. to 4 p.m. each day, except Sundays and Public Holidays [when they shall] be open for gentlemen from daylight to dark.

One of the views on the walk from Bondi to Bronte.

The charge for the baths with use of two towels was 3d with children under 12 half price.

Bronte Beach shelves away quite steeply and usually has boisterous surf, but there's the 'bogey hole' close to the baths which provides safe beach swimming. That end of the beach is naturally rocky and a section has been cleared providing a natural pool with a sandy bottom surrounded by rocks that break the force of the surf.

Forty two acres at Bronte, then known as Nelson Bay, were originally bought by the Colonial Architect Mortimer Lewis in several lots in the 1830s. Lewis was the designer of the Signal Station at South Head, the Treasury building in the city as well as many other buildings in New South Wales and he superintended the erection of Government House from the plans of the English architect, William Blore. At Nelson Bay Lewis embarked on the construction of a colonial house on the hill overlooking the beach, but an economic downturn in the early 1840s led him to sell his entire landholding and the uncompleted house to Robert Lowe in 1843. Lowe was a barrister who had arrived in Sydney the previous year. He was an albino with the characteristic white hair, pink eyes and light coloured skin of that genetic peculiarity and wore thick dark glasses with close fitting leather shields to prevent stray light entering his eyes. He completed Lewis' house where he lived with his wife and used to ride on horseback every day into the city to his Chambers and to fulfill his duties at the Legislative Council where he'd been appointed as a member on the recommendation of Governor Gipps. Mrs Lowe wrote to her mother about the house:

> We have a little estate of 42 acres, four miles from Sydney, on the sea; it is lovely beyond conception. We have given only £420 for it ... We are furnishing the house ... The scenery resembles Jersey, but is far more beautiful – the vegetation is so lovely. We have a beautiful bay to ourselves. The trees line the shores, with drives through them; we have a waterfall of 60 feet, and this runs through a fine gully. It is a most romantic spot, and just suits my tastes.

Mrs Lowe laid out the garden where she created a maze and had a separate section in the grounds for growing vegetables, once writing to Mrs Sherbrooke in England in 1847

> I have just been planting some seeds that were collected on Dr Leichhardt's expedition. A gentleman who accompanied him gave me a few seeds of each new flower which they discovered ...

In a view like this you can see why Bondi is so famous. It's a perfect crescent of sand.

Bondi on a glorious summer afternoon.

The annual Festival of the Winds at Bondi adds a splash of colour to the scene.

At sunrise the colours in the scene are nature's own.

It was from these seeds that Mrs Lowe was credited with planting the first waratahs in Sydney.

During a debate in the Legislative Council in 1847 Robert Lowe threatened that if the 'Price of Crown Lands Bill' was passed unamended he would leave the Colony. The Bill was passed and Lowe and his wife packed up and left. They returned to England where Robert entered the House of Commons in 1852, became Chancellor of the Exchequer in 1868 and was elevated to the peerage as Lord Sherbrooke in 1880. Before he died in Surrey in 1892 a Sydney wit suggested a fitting epitaph:

> Here lies poor old Robert Lowe;
> Where he's gone to I don't know –
> If to the realms of peace and love
> Farewell to happiness above;
> If, happily, to some lower level,
> We can't congratulate the devil.

On the cliff track to Tamarama.

Lowe was so delighted with the verse when he was sent a copy he translated it into Latin.

Mrs Lowe was an artist as well as a gardener and romantic scenes of her house on the heights overlooking the beach survive. The house wasn't called Bronte in those days, the name was given by a later owner, but history shows that the names of Nelson and Bronte are linked. After Nelson's victory at Aboukir in 1798, the King of Sicily bestowed on Nelson the title of Duke of Bronte and made a gift to him of the estates at Bronte in Sicily.

Part of the estate of Bronte House is now Bronte Park next to the beach. B. T. Dowd, the author of The Centenary of the Municipality of Waverley, described the park in the 1950s

> Bronte Park, or "Bronte the Beautiful" as it is sometimes called, is tucked away in a secluded valley behind its beach and sheltered from boisterous winds. It provides the ideal family picnic ground … Neatly painted 'cubby' houses for picnics and abundant shade by Norfolk Island pines, native fig, honeysuckle and other trees all assist the pleasure-seeker. Swings and merry-go-rounds with a good surfing and sun-baking beach and swimming baths provide all that is desired for family enjoyment.

Which is exactly as it is today. Follow the path at the back of the park past the children's playground and it leads after 300 metres to the gully and waterfall mentioned by Mrs Lowe to her mother. Climb the steps by the waterfall and you come out at Bronte House on Bronte Road. A wonderful surprise like a flash of gold in a prospector's pan. The house was bought by Waverley Council in 1948 and is privately leased, but is periodically open to the public. For dates of opening days contact Waverley Council.

Stroll down Bronte Road to return to the beach. On the way you pass a row of shops overlooking Bronte Park and the beach with chairs and tables outside. Every single shop, seven last time I counted, is a café, so an executive decision is required just which one to stop at for a coffee. Take the lower road directly above the beach which follows the old sandstone cutting for the trams. A report by the Department of Public Works in March 1912 on facilities at Sydney's beaches pointed out that the recently opened tram to Bronte passed above the men's changing sheds and it would be

> Difficult for persons dressing and undressing in such a shed to keep out of the range of vision of passengers in the trams … [and further] We are of the opinion that 'sun bathing' as it is called, or lying on the open beach clad in bathing costume, should not be permitted.

Waverley Cemetery

At the top of the cutting two minutes walk on the neatly paved cliff-top path takes you to Waverley Cemetery. It is the Pere Lachaise of Sydney, the last resting place of many famous Australians. But whereas the Pere Lachaise is in a rather dingy corner of Paris, Waverley Cemetery has an uplifting aspect on a hillside that slopes up from a low cliff above the shimmering blue Pacific. You don't need to go to the Louvre to see sculpture either, some of the white marble carved figures on the headstones at Waverley are just beautiful. If you have time walk through the cemetery to the pavilion on the corner of St Thomas Street and Trafalgar Street, where the location of 35 or so 'historic graves' are listed. Somehow it isn't

There's nothing like a stroll by the ocean to blow away the blues. The track from Bondi to Tamarama.

Bondi Baths is home of the famous 'Bondi Icebergs' club. Once a year in mid-winter members fill the pool with ice-cubes, grit their teeth, and go for a ritual bathe.

the elaborate headstones of Governors, Prime Ministers and Archbishops which you are drawn to, but the simple ones of more humble Australians. Henry Lawson is buried here. His epitaph reads

> Love hangs about thy name like music round a shell.
> No heart can take of thee a tame farewell.

His wife, Bertha outlived him by 35 years. Also buried in the cemetery is Fanny Durack. She once held every world freestyle women's swimming record from 100 yards to one mile. If you don't have time to loiter, the grave of Dorothea Mackellar is near the cliff-top path at the north east corner of the cemetery behind a memorial like a small white marble Acropolis in memory of Sir James Martin a one time Australian Prime Minister. Dorothea's headstone stands next to that of her father, Sir Charles Kinniard Mackellar, who was a member of the New South Wales Legislative Assembly in the nineteenth century. A second inscription on the grave of 'Isabel Marion Dorothea Mackellar' tells us that her brother, Keith Kinniard Mackellar, a 2nd Lieutenant in the Dragoon Guards, was killed 'in the 20th year of his age' at Onderstepoort in July 1900 during the Boer War.

Clovelly

Continue on the cliff track past Tamarama Bowling Club next to Ocean Street and round Burrows Park to Clovelly Bay where an opening in the rocks looks like the exit of the Panama Canal into the ocean. Upstream where you expect maybe a lock is the long thin strip of sand of Clovelly Beach.

As a relief work during the Depression the rocks flanking each side of the long narrow bay were covered with concrete quays. The intention was to close the mouth of the bay with a causeway crossed by a scenic road to create an Olympic Pool, but the work was abandoned in 1938 after the construction was demolished by a storm.

In 1834 William Greville, a clerk in the Colonial Secretary's Department, bought 20 acres including the beach at 'Little Coogee', as it was then known, for £40. The name of the beach was changed in 1914 when the local progress association suggested naming it after Clovelly in Devon.

If you've walked from Bondi you can be excused for stepping into the Clovelly Hotel on Clovelly road near the beach to have a beer and admire the art-deco interior.

Continuing on our trek, we pass the enormous sea of tarmac on the headland next to Victory Street which is the car park for Clovelly and pick up the track again at the entrance to Gordons Bay. This is the site of the 'Gordons Bay Underwater Nature Trail', 620 metres long, used by scuba divers to view the marine plants and animals in the bay. Its route is outlined by a chain held to the seabed by twenty five 44 gallon drums filled with concrete. The walking track rounds the sandy beach at Gordons Bay on a high raised board walk then the route follows Major Street before becoming a track once more as it follows the cliff top in Dunningham Reserve before dropping down to Coogee Beach at the Coogee Palace on Beach Street.

Coogee

Coogee has been a beach destination since the 1820s, when walkers made the hike from South Head, trespassing on the way through William Roberts' Bondi Estate. As a seaside village Coogee was the first in Sydney, 20 years before Manly and 45 years before settlement took place at Bondi. Following a survey of the area land was offered for sale in the 'Township' of Coogee in the New South Wales *Government Gazette* on 1st August 1838. The town plan, which could be viewed at the Surveyor General's office in Sydney, laid out the basic Coogee street grid and reserves which exist today, the street names included 'Neptune', 'Dolphin', 'Fish' and 'Whale' to reflect its seaside location. Dolphin and Neptune Streets survive, though Fish and Whale Streets were renamed respectively Arcadia Street and Coogee Bay Road.

Coogee was Sydney's seaside destination. The tram reached there in 1883, eleven years before it was extended to Bondi, and when passengers requested an early morning tram to Bondi for swimmers the company initially declined on the grounds that it would take patrons away from the already existing early service to Coogee. In 1887 on the north side of the beach a structure, called funnily enough, 'The Bondi Aquarium' opened. Under its central dome was a large dance floor surrounded by the aquarium's collection of strange fish displayed in large tanks. A nearby 'Canadian Toboggan Rink' had wooden trolleys that ran on a wooden dipper down the side of the hill for 150 feet 'adapted to the exigencies of

Tamarama.

Tamarama sunrise.

Bronte House, the first built in the district, once had the beach and 40 surrounding acres for its front garden.

Right page: From bottom of picture, Bronte, Tamarama and Bondi Beaches. Bronte Bogey Hole, at lower right, has become a paddling pool at low tide.

Bronte sunrise.

Tamarama for two? The beach front café.

Looking south from Tamarama.

Bronte Beach.

Looking north from Coogee Beach.

Bronte Baths.

Waverley Cemetery.

Clovelly

city life and a snowless climate … the first that has been erected in the Colonies.'

Early Australians, most of whom had come out from England or were from English backgrounds, were trying to create at their seaside the ideal English holiday resort, and nowhere did they succeed better than at Coogee. On 24th July 1926, long after the era of pier building in England was over, the first pile for the Coogee Pier was driven before a large crowd. The pier opened in 1928, and the following year the Coogee Advancement League published a promotional book *Coogee Australia's Most Beautiful Seaside Resort*, which trumpeted:

> Those who have charge of this beautiful gift of Nature to the Australian people have done everything in their power to make Beautiful Coogee a real holiday-maker's Mecca … the main reason why Coogee today is the Premier Beach of Australia … [is] the Ocean Promenade Pier, which extends from the centre of the seawall straight out into the Pacific for many hundreds of feet … photographs of Coogee Bay … as well as verbal descriptions, cannot adequately convey the sensation of being able to walk on a smooth, clean and dustless deck only a few feet above where the waves of the ever-restless Pacific are pounding on the beach. The thrill of being actually a participant in this conquest of Nature by man must be experienced to be understood …

Gordon's Bay.

The pier, leading directly off the promenade at the end of Coogee Bay Road, was brilliantly lit at night by 12 main lamps and 3,000 smaller bulbs and advertised 'Dancing nightly from 8 p.m. … Sunday afternoon and evening concerts by a magnificent orchestra of thirty performers assisted by popular vocalists and other special acts.' Entry was adults 6d, children 3d.

In the Coogee Advancement League's book was a council advertisement drawing your attention to the fact that

> Coogee possesses the only Shark Proof ocean surfing beach in Australia. Day and Night Surfing. Brilliant sea front lighting recently installed at great cost.

The net stretched across the southern section of the bay to the pier, then back to the beach. At the 'inauguration' of the net in 1929 before a crowd of 135,000 a rope holding back 10,000 swimmers was dropped and they swarmed like a wave into the surf. The cost was a penny to swim within the enclosure though some swimmers still used the north unnetted section of the beach which became known as 'Scotsman's End.'

Coogee's Baths

For those that preferred a pool to the ocean, there were the rock baths on the beach and Giles Baths for Gentlemen on the north headland for 'the Man who wants to keep fit', offering Turkish baths, massage, a gym and sunbathing. Also, on the flat rocks just south of the beach, there were 'McIver Baths for Ladies and Children and 'Wylie's Continental Baths' for mixed bathing.

These worn pillars by the water instantly identify the location for any eastern suburbs resident as Coogee rock pool.

Previous pages: Surf Carnival at Coogee

The contractors for the pier claimed 'Coogee Pier will be considerably stronger than any similar pier constructed in England … NO STORMS WILL EFFECT IT.' I wonder if they are still in business because Pacific storms did affect it and it was dismantled in 1933. The shark net proved more durable though it too was damaged by storms and taken down in 1945. As you strolled through Dunningham Reserve on the way to Coogee you may have noticed that the red brick Giles baths with its orange tiled roof is boarded up and derelict. The Coogee Palace on Beach Street is the renovated 1887 Aquarium, though beneath the dome these days fish are for the patrons of the Regal Pearl Chinese Restaurant. Stroll along the beachfront past the cafés and backpackers' lodges to the track through Grant Reserve and you pass McIver Baths, which since 1886 has been a 'women only' pool. A short distance further along Wylie's Baths were established in 1907 by H. A. Wylie, a champion long distance swimmer. His daughter Mina won a silver medal for swimming at the 1912 Olympics in Sweden. Mina lived in a house nearby at 7 Neptune Street.

As you continue on the track around Trenerry Reserve you'll notice a reef off shore known as Wedding Cake Island after the 'icing' of bird droppings that cover the rocks. Weather permitting, returned servicemen visit the island for a barbecue on Anzac Day.

Maroubra

It's about an hour's walk along the coast and through the backstreets of South Coogee to Maroubra Beach, or a pleasant five minute drive via Arden Street, Malabar Road and Maroubra Road.

Maroubra, Aboriginal for 'like thunder' was always isolated compared with beaches like Bondi and Coogee. The first permanent structure was the woolwash near the beach established in the 1860s where the men lived in tents and bark huts. The steam-engine fires burnt through the night and their glow became a landmark for passing ships. The trams reached Maroubra in 1921 and it was the massive Crown Land sales of the 1920s and 1930s that established Maroubra as a residential suburb. In that era Maroubra's greatest claim to fame was the 'Olympic Speedway' opened in 1925, which was situated on land at the corner of Anzac Parade and Fitzgerald Avenue. The banked concrete racetrack was on the scale of England's famous Brooklands or Indianapolis in the U.S. and attracted Sydney's biggest sporting crowds of the day with attendances of up to 75,000. Five fatalities in short succession including Reginald 'Phil' Garlick one of Australia's best known racing drivers who was killed instantly when his Alvis left the track on the steep north banking was one of the factors that led to the closure of the track just three years later. Maroubra Speedway re-opened briefly as a motorcycle only track before closing for good in the 1930s.

The serious business of having a good time at the beach. Coogee promenade.

Maroubra Beach is still relatively undeveloped. Maroubra Surf Life Saving Club is built on the beachfront at the north end of the beach while the South Maroubra Club overlooks sand dunes. The men of Maroubra Surf Club were in the past well-known for their prowess at rugby. In 1913 club members provided six of the eight forwards in the New South Wales Rugby team. Most of the land on the headland south of the beach is occupied by the Anzac Rifle Range, which was established as a range during the First World War. These days as well as the army the range is used by the Corrective Services Department and various private shooting clubs.

Long Bay

From the city it's a relaxing 11 kilometre drive via the new tunnel past Moore Park (where Fox Studios may be worth a visit on another day) along Anzac Parade to Long Bay. Passing the soccer and cricket grounds and the golf course in Moore Park, then through the built up suburbs of Kingsford and Randwick, Anzac Parade splits into a dual carriageway separated by a wide grassy reserve for the last few kilometres before the forbidding walls of the gaol announce the arrival at Long Bay. It seems hard to believe today but the little beach at Long Bay was once a picnic and weekend resort for people from the city. Four hundred acres of reserves were in the trusteeship of the residents including tree-lined Long Bay Park behind the beach. There were tea and refreshment rooms and Dudley's and Anderson's amusement pavilions on the bay. In the 1850s fox hunts led by the Governor Lord Fitzroy took place in the surrounding countryside.

A good way to start the day, with an early morning swim and run on Coogee Beach.

Long Bay was one of the first place names to be bestowed on the southern beaches, Governor Phillip noting the presence of a 'Long Bay' on an exploratory journey north of Botany. The first gaol at Long Bay was the State Reformatory for Women, opened with 334 cells in 1909 including an asylum for 'female inebriates.' The gaol was situated at Long Bay in the hope that the fresh air and spacious setting with its outside farm would provide a conducive atmosphere for rehabilitation of inmates. This was followed by the opening of the State Penitentiary for men at Long Bay in 1914. At the request of local residents who didn't want their suburb to be associated for evermore with a gaol, the name was changed to Malabar in memory of the steamship of that name which ran on to the rocks on the northern headland of the bay in a thick fog on 2nd April 1931.

Little Bay

Forty minutes walk around the coast from Long Bay past Randwick Golf Course takes you to the more picturesque and even more isolated Little Bay. In 1881 victims of a smallpox outbreak in Sydney were isolated at a 'Sanitary Camp' at Little Bay. It was literally a camp, of canvas bell tents above the beach, using the nearby stream as a freshwater supply. Following further outbreaks of smallpox and typhoid the Government established the permanent Coast Hospital at Little Bay. The region was still remote, 12 kilometres on an unsealed road from Sydney and thought far enough from the centre of population 'to ensure safety and confidence' for an isolation hospital. As well as treating cases such as tuberculosis, diphtheria, measles and scarlet fever the hospital had a 'Leprosarium' where a permanent population of 30 or 40 lepers were confined by law as leprosy was then an incurable disease.

When junior comes along it may be just an early morning walk.

With the end of the great epidemics in the 1930s the hospital was renamed the Prince Henry in 1934 in honour of the visiting Duke of Gloucester and expanded into a teaching hospital specialising in more traditional fields of medicine.

As you leave the hospital you'll notice a clock on a brick clock tower. The face and mechanism was made at Blenheim in Germany in 1878 and brought to Australia for the Sydney International Exhibition of 1882.

Henry Head Bushwalk

Continue south on Anzac Parade, turn left on Bunnerong Road then left again just past Grose Street on the road that leads through the bush to the New South Wales Golf course. Don't take the turn-off for the golf club, but continue east and stop at a gate where a track leads to the Coast Hospital Cemetery. On a windswept bleak site like a scene out of Great Expectations stand the gravestones of patients and nurses who died of infectious diseases at the old hospital.

From the cemetery, it's a three hour round trip by foot via Henry Head, La Perouse and Anzac Parade back to the car, but there are enough places of interest on the way to make a half day of it. Continue on the sealed road past the Sydney Pistol Club and take the track towards the old concrete buildings on the hill. These are the remains of the extensive

Surf carnival at Maroubra.

Nature's sculpture. Rock forms on the walk from Coogee to Maroubra.

defence works erected at 'Cape Banks Fort' during the Second World War. As well as long range coastal guns, anti-aircraft guns and torpedo launching facilities there were plotting rooms, a barracks, a military hospital and an electricity generating plant.

Past the fort a pedestrian bridge crosses a rocky gully to Cape Banks. The green for one of the holes of the N.S.W. Golf Course is on the Cape, and golfers chip over the gully then walk over the bridge to the hole. On the rocks below are the rusting remains of the *Minmi*, a coastal steamer which was wrecked on Cape Banks during a fog in May 1937. Fresh water pools directly below the 18th tee of the N.S.W. Golf Club are believed to be those noted by Captain Cook in the log of *H.M.S. Endeavour*.

Re-cross the pedestrian bridge and continue west around the coast to the fortifications and 'Endeavour Light' at Henry Head. Henry Head Fort is older than that at Cape Banks, the first gun emplacements were built at the end of the nineteenth century. A short distance further is Little Congwong Beach, an unofficial nudist beach, then another ten minutes walk takes you to Congwong Bay Beach, which has a view of nearby Bare Island Fort and across Botany Bay to Kurnell. A short climb up the track at the east end of the beach takes you to La Perouse.

La Perouse

According to a plaque on a monument next to the car park at nearby Yarra Bay, 'In this vicinity, about 3 p.m. on 18th January 1788, Governor Phillip first set foot on Australian soil.' Phillip had arrived at Botany Bay two days ahead of the rest of the First Fleet. According to the journal of Phillip Gidley King 'we came to an anchor on the Northern side of the Bay, that the ships which were following might not miss the harbour.' Phillip spent most of that afternoon searching for fresh water, until finally, according to Surgeon James Callam's account, 'near sunset', some natives

> Conducted us to a delightful rivulet of Spring Water, which emptied itself in the Bay close by us; – here we partook of the pleasing stream, drank success to the Colony, and the Speedy arrival of the Fleet.

The rest of the First Fleet entered the Bay and were preparing to sail for Sydney Harbour on the 24th of January when the sighting of two strange ships on the horizon caused some consternation, Captain Watkin Tench of the marines believing 'They were Dutchmen sent to dispossess us.' Phillip hurriedly ordered the English colours to be hoisted on the south point of the bay. In fact the ships weren't Dutch, but French, and two days later when the ships were off the entrance to the bay as Captain Hunter of the *Sirius* recalled

> I sent a boat with an officer to assist them in and, about one hour after, a breeze sprung up from the S.E. and they were safely anchored in the bay.

Phillip took the First Fleet to Sydney leaving the French to their own devices at Botany Bay. Here they camped for six weeks and built a stockade on the point now known as La Perouse after the commander of the expedition, Jean-Francoise de La Perouse. La Perouse was in command of two frigates, the *Boussole* and *Astrolabe*, on a voyage of scientific exploration and discovery in the Pacific under the enthusiastic support of King Louis XVI of France. Two months earlier, in the Samoan Islands, eleven men from the expedition were massacred by natives and many others wounded. One of these wounded men, the expedition Chaplain, Father Receveur, died at La Perouse and was buried under a eucalyptus tree. Before leaving, La Perouse left with Phillip his reports and some letters to be sent to France by the first available ship. On sailing from Botany Bay La Perouse's expedition was never heard of again. It wasn't until nearly forty years later that the Irishman Peter Dillon, a captain with the East India Company, established that La Perouse's ships had been wrecked on the island of Vanikoro.

On climbing the steps of the guillotine on 21st January 1793, Louis XVI was asked if he had any final words and he enquired 'At least, is there any news of Monsieur de La Perouse.'

The best day to visit La Perouse is a Sunday, when snake-handlers give demonstrations in an enclosure next to Anzac Parade. Exhibitions of snake-handlers have been a tradition at La Perouse ever since 'Professor' Frederick Fox showed his prowess at handling the reptiles at the tram loop in 1911 using snakes collected in the Botany and La Perouse area. Nearby, aborigines demonstrate their boomerang throwing skills and offer boomerangs for sale. Aborigines have had a long association with the area, they were here for thousands of years before European settlement and Cook's, Phillip's and La Perouse's expeditions all recorded encounters with the 'natives.' A 'Reserve for the use of Aborigines' was established at La Perouse in the 1880s run by missionaries, the 'La Perouse Aborigines Christian Endeavour Society.' They even had their own newspaper, *The Aborigines*

Maroubra, just as spectacular a beach as Bondi, but the world seems to have passed it by.

Sunrise, Mahon Pool, Maroubra.

Surfers at Maroubra.

Congwong Bay Beach and Little Congwong Beach from La Perouse.

Advocate. A tiny Mission church was built on the sand dunes near the beach at Frenchmans Bay. It was moved to more stable ground and still stands today on the corner of Elaroo and Adina Streets.

On the centre of the grassy headland of La Perouse you may have noticed a small sexagonal sandstone tower, all that survives of a Watch House built by Macquarie to look out for smugglers and the entry of 'strange vessels' into Botany Bay. The tower, built in 1820-21, is one of Australia's earliest colonial buildings.

A little further across the grass a large burgundy coloured building is the old Cable Station, erected in 1882 for the 'Australasian and China Telegraph Company.' The Station relayed and received messages on the 1,580 mile eastern extension of the cable to New Zealand. If the public wished to use the service the cost was nine shillings for ten words. When the station became disused it went through a variety of uses including a Salvation Army refuge for women and children before being re-opened as the La Perouse Museum in 1988. The museum, open Wednesday to Sunday, takes you on the fascinating journey of La Perouse's expedition and includes a display of relics from his ships recovered from the reef at Vanikoro. As you come out of the museum, on the right is Father Receveur's grave, maintained by the Franciscan Order. Nearby on the left, is the monument to La Perouse.

Bare Island

On the point a sturdy wooden bridge leads to Bare Island Fort, open for tours on Saturdays and Sundays. The island was given its name by none other than the venerable Captain Cook, whose advice to future mariners on entering Botany Bay was

> To sail into it keep the South Shore on board until within a small bare island which lies close under the North Shore.

The island was fortified in the 1880s with five gun emplacements connected by bombproof passages leading to a barracks, magazines and a command post. Declared redundant as a defence installation in 1902, in 1912 the buildings of the fort became a retirement home for war veterans, the first residents being mostly English veterans from European wars some of whom had served in the Crimea. The home was run by a committee of voluntary women workers belonging to the British Empire League. Men were given a navy blue uniform with brass buttons and a red stripe down the trousers, and caught the tram into the city (for which they were given a free ticket) to form a Guard of Honour at ceremonies such as Empire Day and Anzac Day. The home functioned for the next 50 years, except for a short period when the island was re-fortified during the Second World War. Bare Island became a Historic Site in the 1960s and in 1984 was incorporated into Botany Bay National Park. Return to the car by Anzac Parade and the road to the golf links.

On leaving La Perouse by Bunnerong Road you pass the sprawling Botany Cemetery on the left. Near the entry to the cemetery on Koorooera Avenue is the Pioneer Memorial Park containing the headstones of early settlers salvaged from the old Devonshire Street Cemetery in 1901 when the ground was used to build Central Railway Station. The gravestones preserved include those of John Cadman, Mary Reiby, Simeon Lord and bushranger, John Dunn. Turn left on Botany Road past the enormous Port Botany Container Terminal. Botany Bay is the busiest port in New South Wales, eclipsing even Sydney Harbour.

Mascot Airport

Continuing on Foreshore Road and turning left on General Holmes Drive, the road dives through a long tunnel below the two north-south runways of Kingsford Smith Airport, Australia's busiest airport. The airport was the idea of Nigel Love, a returned pilot who fought in the First World War. By 1924 interstate flights were operating and fourteen years later in 1938 the airport had a staff of eleven and three gravel landing strips. When the airport entered the jet-age and the first north-south runway was built, a sewage farm, a racecourse, a gun club, sports fields and a golf course were bulldozed and the course of the Cooks River diverted.

Brighton-le-Sands

After driving over the Endeavour Bridge at the mouth of the Cooks River the road follows the shore of Botany Bay for several kilometres past the suburbs of Brighton-le-Sands, Monterey, Ramsgate Beach and Sans Souci. Brighton was put on the map in 1886 when local entrepreneur Thomas Saywell opened the sixty room New Brighton Hotel overlooking the bay. Nearby was a skating rink and a racecourse and to service his resort

Dawn at Kingsford Smith Airport. The planes are immobile until the lifting of the nightly curfew.

Bare Island Fort.

The monument to La Perouse.

Pines at Cook Park, Botany Bay.

Brighton-le-Sands.

Saywell built a wharf into the bay from which steam ferries plied to Sydney. The ferry wharf overlooked on each side enclosed baths for men and women. A notice by the ladies' bath read 'Blackguards Peep In – Gentlemen Pass On.'

An early pioneer Thomas Holt owned enormous tracts of land south of Sydney in present day Sutherland and had a house called Sans Souci in the suburb which now carries that name. In 1874 Holt hosted a visit to his property by the Governor Sir Hercules Robinson and his wife, who remarked that 'Seven Mile Beach' as it was then known would make a very fine gallop. Holt had the name of the long strip of sand on Botany Bay changed to 'Lady Robinsons Beach.'

In Sans Souci just where the Grand Parade swings round to the right into Sandringham Street a wide band of pine trees lines the shore in Cook Park. The park isn't named after Captain Cook, but after Samuel Cook, a newspaper editor and contemporary of Thomas Saywell who campaigned in the press to have the pines planted as a wind-break and the area preserved as a park.

Captain Cook's Landing Place

At the end of Sandringham Street turn left on Rocky Point road which at Rocky Point crosses the Georges River by the graceful arch of the Captain Cook Bridge. Continue on Taren Point road then turn left on Captain Cook Drive which takes you after 11 kilometres to a 248 acre park at Captain Cook's Landing Place where a National Parks and Wildlife Service Discovery Centre documents Captain Cook's landing at Botany Bay.

Cook sailed into Botany Bay at 2 p.m. on Sunday 29th April 1770. It was his first landfall on the east coast of Australia which Cook had Admiralty instructions

> with the Consent of the Natives to take possession of the Convenient Situations in the Country in the Name of the King of Great Britain.

However when Cook landed with two rowing boats on the rocks just inside the southern headland of the bay two aborigines made a gallant attempt to resist the landing, shouting and throwing spears. Cook's party fired warning musket shots, but when this didn't have the desired effect they fired at the Aborigines, wounding one in the leg, and they ran off into the bushes. Cook stayed for eight days exploring the bay and according to his journal 'During our stay in this Harbour I caused the English Colours to be display'd ashore every day.' Before leaving Australia at Cape York Cook claimed the entire eastern coast for Great Britain.

With Cook on his barque the *Endeavour* was the naturalist Joseph Banks, who the Royal Society had persuaded the Admiralty should be allowed to travel on the voyage to explore the South Seas. Banks contributed £10,000 of his own money for the expedition and took with him a staff of eight, including Dr Daniel Solander, a Swedish naturalist, and two Negro servants. Only four, including Banks and Solander, survived the voyage, the two servants freezing to death during the eastern passage of Cape Horn. During their stay at the bay Banks and Solander collected numerous examples of flora never previously seen by European eyes and when the expedition departed Cook named the location 'Botany Bay' because of 'the great quantity of New Plants & ca Mr Banks and Dr Solander collected in this place.' Cook also named Cape Banks and Point Solander in honour of the naturalists, and Point Sutherland close to where he made his first landfall after seaman Forby Sutherland who died of tuberculosis while the expedition was at Botany Bay and was buried close by.

The first land grant at Kurnell was of 700 acres by Governor Macquarie to Captain James Birnie, who established 'Alpha Farm' there run by a manager. Birnie was later 'pronounced lunatik' and the land holding was sold to a wealthy ex-convict merchant, John Connell. Kurnell is the Aboriginal corruption of John Connell's surname. When Captain Birnie and his wife died they were buried in the Devonshire Street Cemetery and their headstones are amongst those in the Pioneer Memorial Park at Botany Cemetery.

Kurnell became a small island community with the odd farm and fisherman's cottage on Silver Beach connected to the outside world by a ferry to La Perouse and the no '64' bus, which during the 1940s battled through the sand dunes and along the beach from Cronulla. All this changed in 1954 when Captain Cook Drive was completed to service the Kurnell Oil Refinery, one of the largest in Australia, which has the capacity to refine 120,000 barrels of oil a day. The refinery is connected by a submarine pipeline to the Banksmeadow Oil Terminal on the north shore of Botany Bay.

Tourists have been coming to Kurnell since 1870, when Thomas Holt erected a monument to Cook's landing near the shore to mark the centenary of Cook's visit to Botany Bay. Holt had bought Connell's land holdings at Kurnell, along with most of the rest of the land between Botany Bay and Port Hacking. The region subsequently became known as the Shire of Sutherland after Forby Sutherland from the Orkney Islands in Scotland who was the first European to be buried on the east coast of Australia. It's always a pleasure to go to Captain Cook's Landing Place. It's a peaceful spot with acres of lush grass and tree-lined paths winding between the monuments to Cook's voyage and past the little stream which was used to restock the Endeavour's water supply. As you sit on the polished stone bench which is a memorial to Joseph Banks and gaze through the Norfolk Island pines lining the shore to the sparkling water you feel as though you could be on a desert island and the occasional roar of a jumbo taking off from Mascot Airport five kilometres away across the bay could be a whole continent away.

The monument to Cook's landing at Kurnell.

Cronulla

Cronulla, six kilometres long, is Sydney's longest beach. Named in 1827 by Surveyor Robert Dixon, Cronulla is a corruption of the Aboriginal word 'Kurranulla' meaning the place of pink shells after the numerous pink 'pippies' which used to be found on the beach. There are extensive sand dunes at the north end of the beach, which are used to shoot desert scenes in movies, including Charles Chauvel's 1940s epic about the campaign of the Australian Light Horse in Palestine during the First World War 'Forty Thousand Horsemen.' Tens of millions of tons of sand have since been removed from the beach by sandmining, but there was still enough there for the shooting of the desert scenes more recently in 'Mad Max III.'

Thomas Holt

The Sutherland district was sparsely populated in the early days because travel to Sydney meant crossing the broad channel of the Georges River. In 1861 the total population of Sutherland was 34 males and 31 females living in eight houses and four tents. It was about that time that activity in the district received a boost when Thomas Holt started purchasing land there. Holt, a Yorkshire wool buyer, was inspired to travel to New South Wales after reading Dr J. D. Lang's *Historical and Statistical Account of the Colony*. After his arrival in 1842 Holt became a successful wool trader and land speculator, his holdings including the so-called Holt-Sutherland Estate, which by the 1880s covered 12,000 acres, from Botany Bay to the Georges River and from Port Hacking to the Woronora River. Holt built several homes in Sydney, including Sans Souci; a 39 room mansion 'Sutherland House' on the shore at Sylvania, and 'The Warren' at Marrickville, where to the anguish of Australian farmers ever since, Holt introduced 60 wild rabbits to hunt in the grounds. On his

Captain Cook's Landing Place on Botany Bay. These flat rocks were the first place where Europeans stepped ashore on the east coast of Australia.

Cronulla is one of the boom areas of Sydney, with new apartments squeezed on to the peninsula between Gunnamatta Bay and the ocean.

Most of Cronulla Beach is still wind-swept sand-dunes.

Sutherland Estate, Holt first tried raising sheep, then cattle, but when these livestock enterprises failed he leased the land to saw millers who cut down the extensive ironbark and blackbutt forests. Miranda was the name given to a sheep farm by James Murphy, the Irish manager of the Holt-Sutherland Estate, after the female character in Shakespeare's play, *The Tempest*.

Surf carnival at South Cronulla.

Sutherland

The first settlement of any size in Sutherland was the little township of that name which sprang up around the railway station when the south coast railway came through in 1885. The nearby Como railway bridge over the Georges River was considered quite a feat of engineering at the time. D. H. Lawrence and his wife crossed the bridge by train in 1922. He wrote in his autobiographical novel *Kangaroo*

> 'Como' said the station sign. And they ran on the bridges over two arms of water from the sea, and they saw what looked like a long lake with wooded shores and bungalows: a bit like Lake Como, but oh, so unlike. That curious sombreness of Australia, the sense of oldness, with the forms all worn down low and blunt squat.

Now the original single track railway bridge has been superseded by a modern concrete structure with lines in both directions, but the old steel bridge still stands next to it and carries a pedestrian and cycle track to connect Como with Oatley. On the Como shore of the river at the end of Cremona Road a boat shed offers motor boats for hire from which you can spend a relaxing couple of hours exploring the Georges River.

But while Sutherland had its little railway township, Cronulla, for the moment, remained deserted. The first resident was Joseph Springall who in 1889 built the 30 room 'Oriental Hotel' overlooking the beach on the northern side of Woronora Road (The Kingsway) to cater for intrepid travellers who made their way to windswept Cronulla. An article in the *Illustrated Sydney News* of that year noted that the hotel offered

> the best of accommodation and food, with exceedingly moderate charges, good sport, beautiful scenery and, in fact, everything which goes to make a holiday one of unalloyed happiness.

Unfortunately for Springall he was ahead of his time, during the early 1890s there was a severe depression in Sydney, visitors didn't flock to his hotel and in his own words he 'lost everything at Cronulla through my business being so unsuccessful and the Building Society closing in and selling the place.' By 1894 Cronulla Beach had a daily mail service and was connected by a 'constructed road' to Sutherland Station, though there were still only 13 on the electoral roll in 1900. This probably represented a population of 50 as women were not then listed on the roll. A 'School of Arts' opened at the fledgeling settlement in 1907, preceding by three years the opening of Cronulla's first school in 1910. The following year Cronulla was really put on the map with the opening of the steam tram service from Cronulla to Sutherland Station. Four years later in February 1915 Cronulla was inaugurated as a surfing beach when Duke Kahanamoku gave a demonstration of surf-board riding at 'Big Beach' (North Cronulla). The *St George Call* reported, he made it look 'so ridiculously easy [by] standing upright, standing on his head, diving off, twisting the board.'

When the Cronulla-Sutherland railway opened in December 1939 it was the first substantial rail construction project in New South Wales for 40 years. Not only is Cronulla Station the only one at a beach in Sydney, it also has at 384 metres the second longest passenger platform in the state to allow for the rapid exit of crowds leaving the beach.

On Gunnamatta Bay just below the station on Tonkin Street, Cronulla Public Wharf is serviced by a ferry which runs to Bundeena on the opposite shore of Port Hacking. Three hour cruises of Port Hacking also depart from the wharf, run by Cronulla and National Park Ferry Cruises Ltd.

Port Hacking

Port Hacking was named by Matthew Flinders after an acquaintance, Henry Hacking, who had told Flinders of the existence of a river south of the Georges River. In 1796, George Bass, his servant, 'boy' Martin and Matthew Flinders set out from Sydney in a tiny rowing boat the *Tom Thumb* to search for the river in question. On 30th March they landed at 'Port Hacking' where they spent two days, Flinders writing:

> Our time was employed in examining Port Hacking and in fishing, occasionally; but finding the port very shoal and but few places in it fit for shipping, we did not think it worth while expending much time about.

Henry Hacking, a quartermaster with the First Fleet was quite a character, a bit like Harry Flashman in the George Macdonald Fraser novels. He stayed on in Sydney after his voyage out with the First Fleet and was one of the first explorers to attempt to cross the Blue Mountains but in 1799 was convicted of perjury and sentenced to transportation to Norfolk Island. Hacking was later pardoned, but while working as a pilot on Sydney Harbour was accused of stealing goods from a vessel and sentenced to death. The sentence was commuted to seven years transportation to Tasmania, where David Collins the Lieutenant Governor gave Hacking a job as a pilot at Hobart. When Governor King in Sydney heard he wrote to Collins 'I am glad you have kept Hacking, he is a good man, but lost here by the Arts of a Woman.' In fact Hacking had shot and wounded the woman in question, for which he had received a reprieve. By the time he retired in 1816 it was because he was 'useless as a Pilot from Drunkenness and other infirmities', though he lived on to the age of 81 and was buried in Hobart in July 1831.

Cronulla Station is a good starting point for the best walk in the area, 'The Esplanade' a six kilometre circuit around the Cronulla Peninsula. There are views of the ocean, Port Hacking, and Gunnamatta Bay and the track skirts six beaches and passes through five parks.

E. G. Waterhouse National Camellia Gardens

A visit to Sutherland wouldn't be complete without a stop at the E. G. Waterhouse National Camellia Gardens at Kareena Road Caringbah. Magnificent in spring and autumn, beautiful in summer and winter, the gardens are worth making a special journey to see, or make a convenient rest stop on the way to or from the south coast. A network of paths wind past little creeks and waterfalls and flower beds containing some 1,500 camellias and 3,000 azaleas. The gardens, established in 1970 to commemorate the bicentenary of Cook's landing at Kurnell, were named after Professor E. G. Waterhouse, a noted world authority on camellias who lived in Sydney.

The Esplanade walking track follows the shore around the Cronulla peninsula.

South Cronulla Beach and rock baths.

Port Hacking.

E. G. Waterhouse National Camellia Gardens, Caringbah.

Sydney Surrounds

The Olympic Stadium, Homebush Bay.

Sydney Surrounds

Heading north out of Sydney on the Pacific Highway, pass through North Sydney, Chatswood and Hornsby and in Berowra take the Berowra Waters Road on the left. After passing through the suburb of Berowra Heights the road is soon passing through bush scenery with views across the valley of Berowra Creek before winding steeply down to the ferry at Berowra Waters. The free car ferry is open 24 hours a day except the first Tuesday of the month from noon to 2.30 p.m. A section of the Great North Walk from Sydney to Newcastle passes through Berowra Waters along the eastern side of the creek. Details of this walk and others in the area are provided by a map next to the path. Most of the houses at Berowra Waters are tucked in the bush on either side of the creek and only accessible by water. Meals are available from various restaurants, including the Berowra Waters Inn, one of Sydney's best-known restaurants, accessed after a very pleasant short trip on a ferry from the marina on the west bank.

Old Northern Road.

Fagan Park

After crossing Berowra Creek on the ferry follow Bay Road and Arcadia Road through picturesque bush and rural scenery. In Arcadia the road passes a Benedictine Monastery on the right and after two or three more kilometres the entrance to Fagan Park is on the left.

One of the great things about Sydney is even if you've been here for 20 years there are still new interesting places to discover. That's how I felt one day in 1999, when on the way to Wisemans Ferry I happened across Fagan Park. Covering 55 hectares, the 'Gardens of Many Nations' in the park surround a landscape of rolling lawns and lakes overlooked by pavillions and little bridges. Each of the eight gardens has plants typical of the style of gardens in Japan, China, England, Holland, the Mediterranean, Africa, the Americas and Australia. The park was established as a Bicentenary project in 1988 by Hornsby Shire Council on former orchards belonging to the Fagan family. After the Fagan family donated the land to the people of New South Wales their house and farm buildings were turned into a rural museum which now forms one section of the park. There are also children's playgrounds, a track for walkers and cyclists and sheltered coin-operated barbecues. Dogs are allowed in the park on a leash. The park is open seven days a week 7 a.m. to sunset. There is a small entry charge through the coin-operated entry gate at the carpark off Arcadia Road.

Wisemans Ferry

A kilometre past Fagan Park turn right on Galston Road and follow Mid-Dural Road to the junction of Old Northern Road. Turn right and follow Old Northern Road through fruit orchards at Glenorie and a sparsely populated bush landscape for 20 kilometres to Hawkins Lookout which has a view of the wooden slopes of the Hawkesbury River Valley from the top of the escarpment. The road then winds steeply down to the small village of Wisemans Ferry perched on the hill above the Hawkesbury river flats.

Governor Phillip first explored the river in June 1789 which he named after Baron Hawkesbury, President of the Board of Trade. Its meandering course still carries the names given by the early surveyors such as Sentry Box Reach and One Tree Reach. The region was a lifeline for Sydney; much of the food needed to support the early colony was grown along the fertile upper river flats on settler's farms manned by indenture convict labour. Once the railway reached Brooklyn in 1888 steamers brought tourists up the river to Windsor who often stayed at Wisemans Ferry overnight.

The little village is named after an early convict settler, Solomon Wiseman. Tried at the Old Bailey for stealing timber from a lighter on the Thames, Wiseman was sentenced to transportation for life to New South Wales and

The English Garden, Fagan Park.

Berowra Waters ferry.

The Mediterranean Garden, Fagan Park.

arrived in Sydney in August 1806 on the convict transport *Alexander* accompanied by his wife and two young sons. Though exiled to New South Wales he was free to pursue his own interests and founded a business carrying coal from Newcastle, timber from the Shoalhaven in a fleet of his own ships. Wiseman obtained his first land on the Hawkesbury in 1817, eventually expanding his holdings to 440 hectares. The land he owned included 'Lower Portland Head' as Wisemans Ferry was then known, where Wiseman lived in a large stone house he built on the hill above the river flats called Cobham Hall. After he'd secured the contract to operate the ferry service across the Hawkesbury on the route of the Great North Road, Wiseman was also able to secure the contract to supply food to the convicts labouring on the construction of the Great North Road and liquor and food to surveyors and overseers. Passengers and stock were carried on the ferry at a specified price, while government servants and officials were carried at no charge. Cobham Hall is now the Wisemans Ferry Inn.

The Great North Road

After crossing the Hawkesbury by the ferry, open 24 hours a day except 10 a.m. to 12.00 p.m. the first Thursday of the month, turn left and after 500 metres you'll see a track on the right which leads up the hill. This is the start of a disused 42 kilometre section of the Great North Road, which runs through Dharug National Park between Wisemans Ferry and Mt Manning. The 264 kilometre Great North Road from Sydney to the Hunter Valley was part of Governor Darling's vision of 'fine and all-encompassing roads' in the colony of New South Wales.

The section of the road above Wisemans Ferry, a steep two kilometre climb known as Devine's Hill, is a monument to the sweat and toil of the convicts who built it. During its construction over six months in 1829, over 550 convicts, many of them working in leg-irons, laboured with hand-tools on the hill. Mostly so-called 'hard cases' who had re-offended after transportation, at Devine's Hill, the convicts built stone retaining walls up to 13 metres high reinforced with massive stone buttresses from blocks weighing up to 600 kilos. A channel cut into the rock where the road ran next to the hillside diverted water into 45 stone box-culverts which passed beneath the road to drain the water through openings in the retaining wall. But this enormous labour was largely in vain. Though the section of road from Wisemans Ferry to Mt Manning followed the ridge-line and was the shortest to the Hunter, there was little water and fodder available for horses and stock and travellers tended to take the slightly longer route through St Albans.

It's only a fifteen minute walk up Devine's Hill to see the convict-built buttresses and culverts. From the top there is a view of the tranquil Macdonald and Hawkesbury River

Wiseman's Ferry at Wisemans Ferry.

Stone embankments on the old Great North Road near Wisemans Ferry were built by convict road gangs.

The statue of Solomon Wiseman at Wisemans Ferry. The wheels are from one of the early cable ferries.

What tales could they tell if stones could speak. Devine's Hill on the Great North Road.

Previous pages: The Hawkesbury River at Lower Portland. The Colo River, a tributary which cuts through the wilderness of Wollemi National Park, enters the Hawkesbury in the middle of the picture on the right.

valleys. Return the same way to the car or there's a longer three-hour round trip which follows an earlier road built on the north side of the Hawkesbury. This road was by-passed when Governor Darling travelled this way and declared it was too steep leading to the construction of the alternative route up Devine's Hill. At the top of Devine's Hill turn right at the locked gate and keep on the track along the ridgeline for about an hour and a half. The old road descends steeply down the hillside by hairpin bends supported in places by stone walls before reaching the Wisemans Ferry Road from where it is a 2½ kilometre walk to the right back to the base of Devine's Hill.

St Albans

From the base of Devine's Hill there's a very enjoyable 42 kilometre drive back to Wisemans Ferry. The route follows the 'Forgotten Valley' through a farming landscape cleared by the early settlers to St Albans, then returns along the opposite side of the valley to the Webbs Creek ferry, open 24 hours a day except 9.30 a.m. to 11.30 a.m. the first Tuesday of the month.

Continue past Devine's Hill heading west on Settlers Road. Six kilometres from Wisemans Ferry, a stone building on the left is the old 'Victoria Inn', built by David and Alexander Cross about 1830-1832. Now a private residence, the inn was also known in the past as the 'You are Welcome Stranger Inn.' After a further 12 kilometres just after the road swings to the right and enters a little patch of woodland the old St Albans Cemetery is next to the road on the left. The cemetery contains many graves of early settlers including William Douglas, a First Fleeter. The cemetery used to be much larger but a large section was washed away by floods.

Another short drive of three kilometres brings you to St Albans, named by an early family of settlers the Baileys after their English hometown. Situated at the head of navigation of the Macdonald River, in its heyday the village had several shops, a courthouse, a police station with a lock-up, an inn, a school and several churches. A flood in 1889 destroyed the courthouse and a new one was built further up the hill. It's now a private residence offering bed and breakfasts. The inn survived the flood, though the water almost reached the ceiling. Known as the Settlers Arms, the inn was first licensed in 1836 and the present sturdy two storey stone building was built about 1848. It's sacrilege not to stop for a drink at the inn while in St Albans, which also offers motel style accommodation at the rear.

Crossing the bridge over the Macdonald River turn left onto St Albans Road which follows the west side of the river through secluded rural scenery and grass river flats. After 10 kilometres glance up the hillside on the right to the walls of St Josephs Church. Now

The Settler's Arms, St Albans.

Pastures in the MacDonald Valley.

The ruins of St Joseph's Church in the 'Forgotten Valley'.

only a shell, the foundation stone of the church was laid in 1839 by Bede Polding, the first Catholic Bishop of Australia. A bush fire destroyed the roof and interior in the 1880s. Just before reaching the Webbs Creek ferry a house on the right is an old butter factory, built in 1908 to process cream produced on the local dairy farms.

NORTH WEST

Crossing the Harbour Bridge out of Sydney, stay on the Warringah Freeway and Gore Hill Freeway into Epping Road then pick up the start of the M2 Motorway at North Ryde. Take the Pennant Hills Road turn off heading north and turn left onto Castle Hill Road. Koala Park Wildlife Sanctuary is a short distance along on the right. The park is something rather special, because it was created as a sanctuary not as a zoo at a time when koalas and other wildlife were being shot in Sydney for their fur. Established as a sanctuary in 1920 by Noel Burnett, the first visitors were coming through in 1926 and it opened to the public as a park in 1930. When Noel Barnett died his daughter took over the running of the park and it is her descendants, the McNamaras, who still run the park today. There are some 55 koalas roaming free among the eucalypts in the park, as well as wombats, echidnas, emus, kangaroos and wallabies. Also in the park are several aviaries and a separate enclosure for the carnivorous dingoes. Koala Park is open seven days a week, with koala feeding times at 10.20 a.m. 11.45 a.m. 2.00 p.m. and 3.00 p.m.

Rouse Hill House

Continue on Castle Hill Road, turn left onto Old Northern Road, right at Showground Road and right again at the junction of Windsor Road. Rouse Hill House is about 9 kilometres along Windsor Road on the left.

Richard Rouse, son of an Oxfordshire cabinet-maker and shopkeeper, arrived in Sydney as a free-settler in 1801. Appointed Superintendent of Public Works and Convicts in Parramatta, Rouse was granted 450 acres near Windsor where in about 1813 he started construction of a house using assigned convict labour. The house, on a hill with a view of the surrounding countryside, was built close to the tollhouse on the Parramatta to Windsor Turnpike. Rouse moved in with his family and his descendants continued living there through a further six generations.

Rouse Hill House was renovated and expanded over the years, including the addition of spacious stables in 1876 designed by John Horbury Hunt. Over the last hundred years the family's financial circumstances saw the surrounding farmland reduced to a holding of 20 acres, but little was changed or added to the house or the furnishings. The last of the Rouse clan to live in the house, Mr Terry, died in 1999, and the estate was opened to the public under the management of the Historic Houses Trust of New South Wales.

A stroll around the house today is like a stroll through the lives of the seven generations of the Rouse family who lived there. It has a kind of lived-in feel. All the furniture, books, photos and bric-a-brac belonging to the Rouse family are still in the house, while outside an ancient horse-drawn buggy lies in repose beneath an out-building and three or four

Friendly creatures at Koala Park.

Rouse Hill House.

ancient Humber cars are scattered about the yard in various stages of dilapidation. Rouse Hill House is open to the public for guided tours from 10 a.m. to 4.00 p.m. on Thursdays and Sundays.

Windsor

Twelve kilometres further along Windsor Road Fitzroy Bridge over South Creek marks the entry to Windsor. On the north west side of the creek, out of sight of the road, is an 1835 Tollhouse, designed by Colonial Architect Mortimer Lewis. Tolls were levied on the Windsor Road until about 1887.

In 1810 Governor Macquarie created five towns along the upper Hawkesbury, Wilberforce, Pitt Town, Windsor, Richmond and Castlereagh. Castlereagh is now the site of Penrith Lakes and the International Regatta Centre for the Sydney 2000 Olympics. Windsor and Richmond were named after the Dukes of Richmond and Windsor. Windsor was re-named from an earlier settlement called Green Hills on a bluff overlooking the first land grants on the Hawkesbury.

In Windsor, take the second turn on the left which is George Street and park on Thompson Square. The Hawkesbury History Museum on the square offers a brochure with a walking tour of Windsor. Nearby, the Macquarie Arms Inn, built in 1815, is the oldest hotel in Australia still trading in its original building. There are beautiful Georgian fanlights above the Thompson Square and George Street doors. A short walk away, on the other side of Bridge Street in Court Street, is Australia's first purpose-built courthouse, designed by convict Architect, Francis Greenway and constructed 1820-1821. A single-storey east wing was added by Government Architect James Barnet in 1890. The building still functions as a Court of Petty Sessions and hears cases from as far afield as Wisemans Ferry. Five minutes walk away, on The Peninsular off Palmer Street are John Tebbutt's observatories, dating to the late nineteenth century. A picture of them appears on the current $100 note. John Tebbutt's 1845 house called The Peninsular is now a restaurant.

There are a score or more other buildings of historic interest in Windsor, the most significant of which is certainly St Matthews Church on the other side of Windsor in Moses Street. Often considered convict architect Francis Greenway's most outstanding work, the church was first used for worship in 1820. The old churchyard around St Matthews with graves dating to 1810 contains several headstones of First-Fleeters marked with small metal plaques.

Richmond

Take Macquarie Street out of Windsor and turn right on Richmond Road. The road runs parallel to the main runway of the large Richmond RAAF Base. A Tourist Information Centre on Richmond Road offers plenty of pamphlets on Richmond and Windsor and the Hawkesbury region. A long avenue of London Plane trees announces the outskirts of the historic town of Richmond. The little town has its own collection of colonial houses and churches, including St Peters (1841). The interior has a solid cedar gallery and pews, and the oldest tombstone in the graveyard dates to 1809. In the centre of town a cricket pitch surrounded by a white picket fence is on the site of the old market square.

Rail travellers alighting at the Victorian railway platform of Richmond terminus are greeted by the sight of the cricket green as they cross East Market Street outside the station. On the opposite side of the park the field is overlooked by an old timber grandstand.

Without question the most magnificent house in the Richmond area is Belmont, about three kilometres outside North Richmond on the Grose Vale Road. The house was built by Philip Charley, a jackeroo who owned one of the original Broken Hill mining syndicates in the 1880s and is credited with spotting the first trace of silver. Immensely wealthy by his mid-20s, Charley bought the Belmont property in 1891 and assisted by architect George Pitt created an Italianate fantasy house with verandas, a central square tower and turrets guarding the corners. Turning off the road past the gatehouse, then approaching a long palm-tree lined drive, entry to the house from the garden is through a pavilion filled with ferns. The work of the sandstone columns of the central tower and reliefs of the exterior are a tribute to the stonemason's craft. Belmont

Hobartville (1828) near Richmond, a perfect example of Georgian architecture.

The only concession to the 21ˢᵗ century at Richmond cricket green is the lighting.

A house on March Street, Richmond, opposite the cricket field.

The spire of St Andrew's Uniting Church.

173

Houses on Thompson Square, Windsor.

John Tebbutt's Observatory.

A section of the streetscape on North Street, Windsor.

Francis Greenway's Windsor Courthouse.

St Matthew's, Windsor.

Houses at Woolwich on the Hunters Hill peninsula.

The old Garibaldi Inn, Hunters Hill.

is now part of the St John of God Hospital and some of the wards occupy the spacious rooms of the house.

WEST

Heading west out of the city, take the Western Distributor over Darling Harbour and follow the signs for Victoria Road. You are soon crossing the span of the sculptural cable-stayed Anzac Bridge. The bridge spans the channel of Johnstons Bay between Pyrmont and Glebe Island. Glebe Island, now joined to the suburb of Rozelle by land reclamations, was the site of the Sydney Abattoirs for about 70 years from 1852. These days the island is host to a massive grain handling silo and terminal.

Passing through the suburbs of Rozelle and Drummoyne, crossing Iron Cove Bridge (1954) and negotiating 13 sets of traffic lights on the way go up and over the graceful arch of Gladesville Bridge. The bridge's 305 metre span was the longest concrete arch span in the world when it was completed in October 1964. The Gladesville Bridge replaced an old swing bridge opened in February, 1881, which was the first bridge spanning the main channel of Sydney Harbour.

Hunters Hill

As the road forks coming down from Gladesville Bridge, take the right fork signposted for Lane Cove, then a short distance later turn off the highway following the signposts for Hunters Hill. Follow Church Street, Alexander Street and Woolwich Road to Clarke Reserve, a grassy park on the waterfront at Clarke's Point with good views of the harbour. The Woolwich Pier Hotel (1892) at the end of Woolwich Road has a bar and bistro and makes a good spot to stop for a bite of lunch.

Hunters Hill, a peninsular 5 kilometres long and an average of 2 kilometres wide, divides the waters of the Lane Cove and Parramatta Rivers. One of the first landowners in the area was Mary Reiby, who purchased a lot of Crown Land at Hunters Hill in December 1839. Under her maiden name of Mary Haydock, living as an orphan with her grandmother in England, the thirteen year old Reiby was sentenced to seven years transportation for going on a joy-ride on a carthorse without first asking the owner's permission. In Sydney when she was seventeen Mary married a ship's officer, Thomas Reiby, who went on to become a successful shipowner and merchant. When Thomas Reiby died in 1811 leaving Mary to bring up their seven children, she took on and expanded her late husband's business interests and became one of the richest people in the colony. The land she bought at Hunters Hill, opposite Linley Point, had a large native fig tree growing in the grounds, and she named the weekend cottage she built there 'Figtree House.'

In 1841 a 17 year old Frenchman, Jules Joubert, arrived in Sydney travelling as a cadet on a French corvette and found a job at the French Consulate. As Jules later recalled, 'I had made up my mind to settle down, in order to do so, I looked about for some land having a prospective value.' Working with his brother Didier who had arrived in Sydney in 1839, and seventy stonemasons brought out under contract from Lombardy in Italy, the Jouberts bought up land in Hunters Hill and set about building houses from the local sandstone. Many of the 200 or so houses they built, standing in their own grounds surrounded by stone walls, still exist today. Jules Joubert pressed his steam yacht *Ysabel* into service as a ferry to bring residents to and from Sydney. He later became the first Mayor of the Municipality of Hunters Hill while his brother Didier was the first Chairman of Council.

Many of the houses at Hunters Hill have a story behind them. Some carry Aboriginal names, such as Warrawilah, 'swirling waters', Kaota, 'eventide', and Gunagulla, 'sky or heaven.' A wooden house in Yerton Avenue is the only survivor of four Austrian pre-fabricated houses brought out by a French settler Etienne Bordier from the Paris exhibition of 1854. 'Passy' a house built by Jules Joubert in 1858 for the French Consul General Louis Sentis, is the origin of the house used by Barnard Eldershaw in the book 'A House is Built.'

When the Burns Bay Road interchange was built in the 1960s cutting across the western section of Hunters Hill, some of the region's old buildings went with

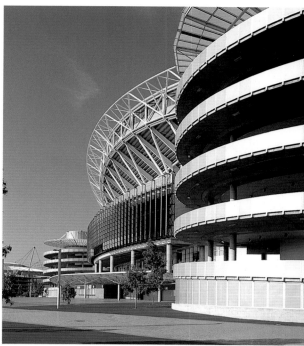

What a difference a century makes. The Olympic Stadium, Homebush.

Are we in Peru or Bolivia? No, it's just the annual Royal Easter Show at Homebush.

Curved shapes and poles make the Homebush Olympic facilities look like a circus or fairground site.

it. Jules Joubert's own cottage, 'St Malo', named after his mother's birthplace in Brittany, was among those demolished. Mary Reiby's house was moved slightly east to make way for the Figtree Bridge, and still occupies a position overlooking the Lane Cove River at Reiby Street. The Anglican All Saints Church dated to the 1850s built in nearby Church Street and known as the 'Fig Tree Chapel', was moved stone by stone to a new site on Figtree Road.

Sydney Olympic Park

Leaving Hunters Hill by the same way you came turn left at Church Street to the Burns Bay Road interchange and after crossing the Tarban Creek Bridge take the fork on the left signposted for Victoria Road and Ryde. Stay on Victoria Road through Gladesville and in Ryde turn left at the signpost for Homebush. Crossing the Parramatta River by the Ryde Bridge stay on the main road on Concord Road and Homebush Bay Drive then turn off for Homebush Olympic Park at Australia Avenue.

A Sydney resident who happens to come this way after ten years in Europe or America would feel the same sense of disorientation as a life-term prisoner coming out of gaol. Everything has changed. Where there were derelict industrial sites, brick pits and State Abattoirs there is now the N.S.W. Tennis Centre, the State Hockey Centre, the Sydney International Aquatic Centre, an Olympic Stadium, the Sydney Super Dome and Sydney International Archery Park. To say nothing of the Showground and pavilions for the Royal Easter Show, an athlete's village with accommodation for 10,000 and the Millennium Parklands, Sydney's biggest urban park, which will have key sections ready in time for the Olympics. Just to put our Sydney resident back in touch with reality at the centre of the

Olympic Park Station, built to handle the tremendous number of visitors at the Sydney Olympics.

Part of the complex of swimming pools at the Olympic Pool.

The Peace Sculpture, Homebush Bicentennial Park.

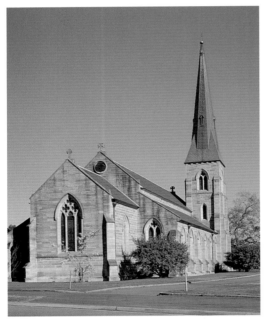

Peace Sculpture of a different kind, All Saints Church, Parramatta.

site on Dawn Fraser Avenue opposite the new Olympic Park station stands the former red brick office of the State Abattoirs with its orange tiled roof.

These facilities are the final chapter of a saga which started on 24th September, 1993 (Sydney time) when at 4.30 in the morning 100,000 revellers at Circular Quay cheered and danced with joy as Juan Antonio Samaranch the President of the International Olympic Committee announced Sydney had won the right to hold the 2000 Olympic Games. The sheer scale of the facilities is just awesome. It's like something from another planet. There are tours of the Olympic site, details are available from the Homebush Bay Visitors Centre on Herb Elliot Avenue, or from the car you can get an appreciation of the main venues. Turn left off Australia Avenue onto Sarah Durack Avenue, and follow Edwin Flack Avenue and Kevin Coombs Avenue to return to Australia Avenue. A far more rewarding alternative is to attend a sports event at one of the stadiums or go for a swim at the International Aquatic Centre, open seven days a week. As well as an Olympic Pool and diving pool the Aquatic Centre has a training pool and a fun pool with a rapid river ride, five spas, a water slide and 'bubble beach.'

Homebush Bicentennial Park

Bennelong Road off Australia Avenue leads to the entrance to Bicentennial Park. Homebush Bicentennial Park was opened on 1st January 1988 as a sister park to Centennial Park, opened exactly 100 years previously. The park, covering 100 hectares of which about 60 hectares are mangroves and saltmarsh, was a rubbish tip in 1983 when the Government embarked on an ambitious project to transform the site into an open grassy landscaped park with lakes, trees, shrubs and barbecue and picnic areas connected by paths for walkers and cyclists. To explore the park a map is available from the Visitors Centre. Points of interest include displays and education facilities in the field study centre, a giant sundial, and the central 'treillage', a viewing tower with a bird's eye view of the park from the top. Talking of birds, a four kilometre return walk or cycle to a small viewing tower at the northernmost point of the park is likely to reward you with a sight of the ducks, pelicans, terns, cormorants and sandpipers that frequent the vicinity. Also well worthwhile is a stroll on the boardwalk running through the grey mangroves.

The Wentworths at Homebush

Before moving on it's worth including a few lines on D'Arcy Wentworth, the first landowner at Homebush. Born in Ireland in 1764, Wentworth served as an apprentice surgeon before leaving for London to complete his studies. In England, Wentworth was twice arrested for highway robbery and twice discharged for lack of evidence. To keep him out of trouble friends arranged to have him appointed assistant surgeon on the convict transport *Neptune* on the Second Fleet. Arriving in Sydney in June 1790, Wentworth applied to Phillip for a post as a Government Medical Officer. He was accepted and sent as the resident surgeon to Norfolk Island penal colony, where he remained for six years with his wife, Catherine Crawley, a convict woman he had met on the *Neptune*. They had three children. The eldest, William, born soon after their arrival in Norfolk Island, was conceived on the voyage out from England on the *Neptune*.

When D'Arcy returned to Sydney in 1796 he was appointed resident medical officer at Parramatta where he also later served as a magistrate. In 1806 D'Arcy received a land grant of 920 acres on the harbour east of Parramatta where he built a house called 'Home Bush.' He would ride to Parramatta or Sydney as business demanded on the back of one of his horses, bred from livestock imported from South Africa and India housed in the stables on the property. In the first horse race held in Sydney at Hyde Park in October 1810, William Wentworth won the race on one of his father's horses.

Parramatta

Returning to Homebush Bay Drive and after two minutes drive turn onto the M4 Motorway for Parramatta. Turn off the motorway, after seven kilometres onto James Ruse Drive to take you into Parramatta.

In April 1788 Governor Phillip set out from Sydney Cove by boat to travel to the navigable limit of Sydney Harbour in search of land for a farming settlement. He chose a site close to the tidal limit of the harbour at a place he named 'Rosehill' after George Rose, Secretary of the Admiralty. Six months later, on 2nd November 1788, accompanied by the surveyor Baron Alt, eleven marines and ten convicts, Phillip camped at Rose Hill and set to work clearing the ground and marking out the streets for a new settlement. Within two years a farm had been established planted with 200 acres of cereal crops, forty one huts each housing 12 convicts had been built, as well as, according to Captain Watkin Tench, 'several small huts where convict families of good character are allowed to reside.' The Governor had a 'lath and plaister' house, and other buildings were under construction using bricks from a kiln which employed 52 convicts and produced 25,000 bricks a week.

The Aborigines called the head of the harbour where a stream cascaded over some broad flat rocks 'Parramatta' meaning 'the place where the eels jump.' In honour of the Aboriginal name Phillip changed the name of his settlement from Rose Hill to Parramatta in June 1791. Parramatta became for a time a bigger town than Sydney, with a population of 1,970 in 1792 compared with only 1,170 in Sydney. As Watkin Tench wrote, 'Sydney has long been considered as only a depot for stores … and all our strength transferred to Rose Hill.'

Elizabeth Farm at Rosehill near Parramatta, the oldest dwelling in Australia.

The City of Parramatta is connected to Sydney by Australia's first train track, opened in 1855. The first ferry on the harbour also ran to Parramatta. Called the *Rose Hill Packet* she was launched in Sydney in 1789 but could take days in unfavourable conditions to make the return journey to Parramatta. The ferry was nicknamed 'The Lump' for being so slow and unseaworthy.

These days the first river-cats connecting Sydney with Parramatta are the best way to travel to Parramatta if not coming by car. The river-cats stop at a wharf near the end of Charles Street. Alighting from the wharf it's a five-minute walk along the south bank of the Parramatta River and across Lennox Bridge to Parramatta Information Centre on Church Street. Lennox Bridge, the first bridge over Sydney Harbour, was designed and built in 1832 by David Lennox a Scottish stonemason. The Information Centre provides a free guide to the many historic buildings in Parramatta, which are open to the public.

Exploring Parramatta

Governor Macquarie's Lancer Barracks at 2 Smith Street, completed in 1820, is still used today by the army. Linden House in the grounds is the museum of the Royal N.S.W. Lancers and displays include trophies, saddlery, weapons and tanks.

The Tudor Gatehouse, Parramatta Park.

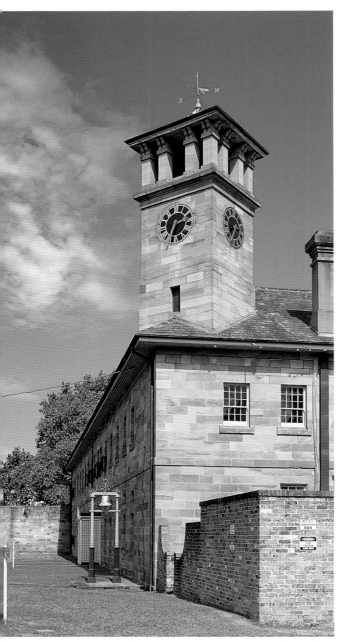

Buildings at Cumberland Hospital, designed by
Government Architect James Barnet, stand on
the site of the convict 'Female Factory'. Inmates
watched the hours grind by on the clock, which
once adorned one of the Factory buildings.

The Soldiers Memorial in memory of servicemen killed in the Boer War stands
on Doric Columns from the 1837 Parramatta Courthouse.

The simple proportions of Government House, Parramatta.

St John's Church stands on Church Street in the centre of
Parramatta.

It must have been a modest Governor who was content with this simple design. Another view of Government House, Parramatta.

In Parramatta Park Old Government House is open seven days a week. It is the oldest public building in Australia and contains the country's finest collection of early Victorian and Georgian furniture. Early governors lived at Parramatta as well as in Sydney. Near Government House is the Governor's Bath House, built for Governor Brisbane in 1823 and the remains of Governor Brisbane's Observatory. A tree stump near the Tudor Gatehouse in Parramatta Park is the remains of the 'Fitzroy Tree' against which Lady Mary Fitzroy, wife of Governor Fitzroy, was thrown and killed when her carriage overturned in Parramatta Park in 1847.

The woollen textile industry in Australia was established in 1801 at the women's convict barracks in Parramatta, where prisoners were put to work spinning and weaving woollen cloth. The barracks, called the 'Female Factory' were nicknamed 'the Black Hole of Parramatta' by the inmates. The mill, employing 1,200 convicts, continued in that role until the 1840s. A high quality tweed the convicts produced was copied by Bradford Woollen Mills in England and is still marketed today as 'Parramatta Cloth.' The remains of the Female Factory buildings are now in the grounds of the Cumberland Hospital off Dunlop Street.

And now for something completely different, Wonderland Sydney.

Coming back to James Ruse Drive on which we arrived in Parramatta if coming by car. James Ruse was the first ex-convict to receive a land grant in March 1791 when Phillip granted him 30 acres as an experiment to see how long a settler took to become self-sufficient starting from an area of uncleared ground. James Ruse later married Elizabeth Perry, the first woman convict to receive her freedom in Australia. Experiment Farm built by First Fleet Surgeon John Harris on Ruse's holding is open to the public on Ruse Street.

Nearby 'Elizabeth Farm' run by the Historic Houses Trust of New South Wales, dating to 1793, is the oldest house in Australia. The furnishings and interior are intended to reflect the mood of the second quarter of the nineteenth century. The house was built by John Macarthur, who arrived in Sydney with his wife Elizabeth in June 1790 with the Second Fleet. Macarthur was a pioneer in establishing and creating an export trade for the merino wool industry in Australia. Granted 100 acres at Parramatta in 1793, Macarthur named the stone farm he built there after his wife. Hambledon Cottage (1824) round the corner in Hassall Street was built by John Macarthur for the retired governess of his three daughters. A Spanish cork tree still standing near the house was planted by Macarthur for corking his locally produced wine.

Wonderland Sydney

Continue west for 15 kilometres on the M4 Motorway through Wentworthville, Pendle Hill, Prospect and Blacktown then at Eastern Creek take the Wallgrove Road turnoff for Wonderland Sydney. Wonderland offers a wonderful day out for the family, with seven theme areas each with its own rides, shows and cafés. Access to all areas of the park, including over 80 rides, is included in the single entry fee. Try the terrifying 'Demon' roller

The first Liverpool Hospital, designed by convict architect Francis Greenway, was built without his supervision after he was dismissed as Government Architect.

coaster or free-fall 'Space Probe 7' in Transylvania if you dare. Wonderland is open seven days a week, 10 a.m. to 5 p.m. If you arrive early the Australian Wildlife Park within Wonderland is included in the entry price and is open 9 a.m. to 5 p.m. The park's collection of Australian native fauna includes enclosures with kangaroos and wallabies, koalas, dingoes, a walk-through aviary of tropical birds, a nocturnal house, and a waterhole with one of the biggest saltwater crocodiles you've ever seen.

SOUTH

Leaving Sydney by Parramatta Road and the M4 Motorway, at Homebush turn left onto Centenary Drive and follow the main road to the start of the M5 Motorway in Beverley Hills. Fifteen kilometres later after passing through the suburb of Moorebank turn off on the Hume Highway for Liverpool.

Liverpool

One of the early landowners on the upper Georges River was Thomas Moore, who obtained holdings in the area by land grants and land purchases in 1805-09. On the morning of 7th November 1810 Governor Macquarie set out from Thomas Moore's home 'Moorebank' in search of a site for a new township. On some rising ground close to the river above flood level Macquarie chose a location 'fit for the purpose' of a town which he called 'Liverpool' after the Earl of Liverpool, Secretary of State for the Colonies. Macquarie immediately instructed surveyor James Meehan to mark out the streets of a settlement. It was the first of the Macquarie towns. In a report on the Colony of New South Wales when he left in 1822 Macquarie mentioned that Liverpool had a schoolhouse, hospital, provision store, barracks, a handsome brick-built church, a gaol and several other government buildings. Macquarie also reported there was a 'wooden wharf or quay, in the centre of the town, to which vessels of 50 tons can come to load and unload, which trade from Sydney to Liverpool by way of Botany Bay.'

After turning off on the Hume Highway for Liverpool, a good starting point for a tour is the Liverpool Regional Museum, 700 metres along on the right. Behind the museum is Collingwood, c.1810, Liverpool's oldest house built by an American whaling captain, Eber Bunker. The house is open for inspection by arrangement with the staff at the museum.

In the centre of Liverpool fifteen minutes walk away are many early colonial buildings, including the church and hospital mentioned by Macquarie. The foundation stone of St Luke's Church on Macquarie Street, was laid by Macquarie in 1818 with the 'active and manly' assistance of his son Lachlan aged four. During its construction the designer, convict architect Francis Greenway, had a dispute with the first building contractor, Nathaniel Lucas, who was found drowned, and the church was completed by

One of the pleasant surprises roaming the outskirts of Sydney is coming across treasures like Collingwood, Eber Bunker's house at Liverpool.

another builder. The old Liverpool Hospital on College Street opposite Bigge Park was also designed by Greenway. Intended to be the main hospital in New South Wales and sited in Liverpool because of the locations' 'pure air and sweet water', the hospital closed in 1853 and became an 'Asylum for Destitute and Infirm Men.' It's worth strolling through the main entry to see some of the old photos inside of the asylum. The old hospital building now houses the Liverpool College of TAFE.

Five kilometres outside Liverpool the convict built Lansvale Bridge over Prospect Creek still carries Sydney bound traffic on the Hume Highway. The graceful sandstone arch of the bridge was opened on 26th January 1836, the 48th anniversary of the founding of the colony, by Governor Burke. As the *Sydney Herald* described the occasion:

> After his excellency had crossed the bridge, twelve dray loads of wool passed over, followed by a cart containing two casks of wine … [and] the ram that won the gold medal at the last meeting of the Agricultural Society, having it placed conspicuously on his forehead. A cart with two emus and a native boy came next…

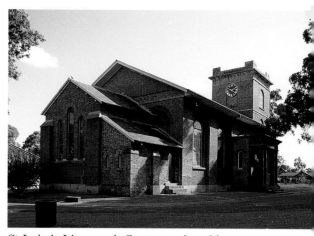

St Luke's Liverpool. Greenway's noble proportions are partially obscured by a hotchpotch of later renovations.

Campbelltown

Outside Liverpool rejoin the motorway for 20 kilometres and turn off on Narellan Road which takes you into Campbelltown, the last of the 'Macquarie Towns', founded by Governor Macquarie on 1st December 1820 in honour of his Scottish wife, Elizabeth Campbell of Airds.

Campbelltown was still a quaint early colonial village in the 1960s like Richmond or Windsor when it rather rudely had foisted upon it one of Sydney's new satellite towns. In Queen Street, the old main road through the village, there's a McDonalds, a Kentucky Fried Chicken and a 24 hour self-service car wash, but also enough early colonial buildings to make an hour or two strolling through Campbelltown a surprisingly rewarding experience.

James Barnet's Courthouse at Campelltown has survived unadorned by unsightly additions.

The best place to get your bearings in Campbelltown is the Quondong Visitor Information Centre on Old Menangle Road at the far south end of Queen Street. The Centre is in the old St Patrick's School, the foundation stone of which was laid by Bishop Polding on St Patrick's Day 1840. Crossing into Queen Street, on the right is Kendall's Millhouse (1843), now containing the Fisher's Ghost Restaurant. In June 1826 Frederick Fisher disappeared in Campbelltown. Four months later, a local farmer, John Farley, saw Frederick Fisher's ghost sitting on a bridge railing pointing to a nearby paddock next to the creek. Local police investigated and found Frederick Fisher's body. Fisher's neighbour, George Worrall, was tried and found guilty of his murder and hanged. The legend lives on in the Festival of Fisher's Ghost held in Campbelltown every year in November.

A little further along Queen Street on the right are a group of four two-storey colonial buildings dating to the 1840s and 1850s including the old Coaching House. On the opposite side of the road the Town Hall (1891) is built on the site of George Worrall's farm where Frederick Fisher disappeared in 1826. The building now houses a theatre and was playing 'Dr Jekyll and Mr Hyde' when I visited. Another five minutes walk along Queen Street, St Peter's Church stands in Mawson Park on the right. On the day I was there doves and pigeons were pecking for bread scraps as the church clock chimed the hour and a game of bowls was in progress on the nearby bowling green. St Peter's was designed and built by Francis Lawless and opened for services in 1823. Frederick Fisher's remains are buried in St Peter's churchyard alongside other notable Campbelltown pioneers. Next to Queen Street in Mawson Park an early sandstone milestone informs us in Roman numerals that Sydney is 33 miles away. Across the road the handsome Victorian structure of Campbelltown Court House was designed by Colonial architect James Barnet.

Mt Annan Botanic Garden

Leaving Campbelltown by Narellan Road, cross the bridge over the motorway and turn left on Mt Annan Drive leading to Mt Annan Botanic Garden. Covering 416 hectares, Mt Annan is the largest botanic garden in Australia, and one of the

English colonial architecture, as at home on the Cumberland Plain as on the plains of India. St Peter's Church, Campbelltown.

Like a movie set. Structures on Queen Street Campbelltown date to the 1840s.

newest, opened in 1988. It is the Native Plant Garden of the Royal Botanic Gardens in Sydney and the intention is that eventually it will display examples of nearly all of Australia's 25,000 known plant species. Roads and cycling and walking tracks wind through the park, which is divided into sections devoted to specific 'themes', including a Rare and Endangered Garden, a Bottlebrush Garden, Wattle Garden and Banksia Garden. There are free gas barbecues and covered shelters in many of the theme gardens. The most rewarding time to visit Mt Annan is in winter and spring for the flowering of the banksias in May, the wattles in July-August, ever-lasting daisies in September and the bottlebrushes in October-November. In the Wattle Garden alone there are over 300 species of Australian wattles. Light lunches and Devonshire teas are served in the garden's café and many of the most picturesque Australian native plants are for sale in pots in the Garden Shop. The park is open seven days a week except for Christmas Day, opening times 10 a.m. to 4 p.m. April to September, 10 a.m. to 6 p.m. October to March.

Thirlmere Railway Museum

Return to the motorway and drive south for a further 22 kilometres to take the Wilton Road turn-off for the little country town of Picton. Thirlmere Railway Museum is about eight kilometres outside Picton via Sanatorium Road. Some of the most interesting steam engines displayed in the giant museum shed include 'No 18' built by Robert Stephenson workshops in the U.K. in 1864. The loco had a working life of 100 years, 32 years on main line freight haulage service then 68 years of shunting duty at the Corrimal Coke Company before being brought to Thirlmere and restored. Also on display is one of the last steam locomotives to enter service in Australia, in 1957, the gigantic Garratt 6040. This model Garratt has 32 wheels and weighs 263 tons. It was the heaviest, longest and most powerful steam locomotive to see service on Australian railways.

Examples of railway passenger cars dating from 1868 are on display. One interesting exhibit is a 1915 prison van. Built to carry 22 'passengers' to country gaols, it also has its own barred prisoner's toilet. Among the freight cars in the museum is one mounted with a device like a giant witch's cauldron used for carrying molten iron in a steelworks.

Return steam train rides operate to Buxton, the next stop up the line, every Sunday and on Sundays and Wednesdays during school holidays. Thirlmere Railway Museum is open 10 a.m. to 3 p.m. weekdays, 9.30 a.m. to 4.30 p.m. school holiday weekdays and 9 a.m. to 5 p.m. weekends and public holidays.

EAST

Head east out of Sydney on the Park Street and William Street, diving through the tunnel beneath Kings Cross then past the yachts bobbing at their marinas on Rushcutters Bay

Cats paws seem ready to embrace the sign welcoming you to Mt Annan Botanic Garden.

Getting up steam at Thirlmere Railway Museum.

Shark Beach at Nielsen Park near Vaucluse House.

and through Edgecliff and ritzy Double Bay on New South Head Road. Stay on New South Head Road through tranquil Rose Bay and up the hill on the other side, turn left on Vaucluse Road just past the towering Convent of the Sacred Heart and follow it into Wentworth Road. After a short distance turn right up the drive and into the car park in the grounds of Vaucluse House.

Vaucluse House

The stately home received its name from the 'Gentleman Convict', Sir Henry Brown Hayes, who is thought to have named it after Fontaine-de-Vaucluse in France, where an underground stream emerges into a steep sided valley in a setting not dissimilar to that of Vaucluse in Sydney. Hayes, an Irish Baronet and Sheriff of Cork, was a 35 year old widower when in 1797 he abducted a Quaker heiress and forced her to marry him. The lady, Miss Mary Pike, was rescued by her friends and Hayes absconded with a reward on his head of £1,000 for anyone lucky enough to capture him. Two years later Hayes walked into the shop of Mr Coghlan, a hairdresser in Cork, and suggested he might turn him in and collect the reward. Three substantial red brick houses built by Coghlan on the reward money are still standing on the Grand Parade, Cork. Hayes was subsequently transported to Australia on the convict transport *Atlas*, arriving in July 1802, where he was permitted by governor King to buy 200 acres of land on the harbour near south Head to establish a farm. Employing fellow convicts to cut down trees and clear the ground, Hayes built a small stone cottage on his holding overlooking a nearby bay and the harbour.

To the consternation of Hayes, the local countryside was infested with snakes, which he was absolutely terrified of. The wife of a major in the N.S.W. Corps made a note of his conversation with Sir Henry and her husband, Sir Henry complaining:

> The brutes, however, have lately taken to invade the house. We have killed them in the veranda, and in every room including the kitchen ... Last night I found a gentleman six feet long, and as black as coal, coiled up on my white counterpane, and another of the same dimensions underneath the bed.

To counter this threat Hayes obtained the permission of the Governor to import a consignment of genuine Irish bog, dug up from the estate of a friend in Cork, instructing 'It shall come out in large biscuit barrels. I shall have a trench dug round the premises, six feet wide and two feet deep.' A shipment of 40 barrels of Irish peat arrived a year later, the Irish superintendent of convicts lending Hayes barrows and shovels and a gang of 75 men to dig the trench. For the ceremony of the filling in of the trench a crowd of ladies and gentlemen travelled out from Sydney to Vaucluse by boat, and after witnessing the spectacle were entertained beneath a tent made of sails lent by the captain of a ship on the harbour.

Pardoned in 1812, Hayes returned to Ireland and Vaucluse was bought by Captain

Vaucluse House.

The grounds of Vaucluse House lead to Vaucluse Bay on the convoluted shoreline of Sydney Harbour.

Juliette feeding the swans at Centennial Park.

A Tommaso Sani statue of a rugby player overlooks the playing fields at Centennial Park.

John Piper who reckoned that no snakes were ever seen within the 'magic circle' of earth.

A subsequent owner of Vaucluse House was William Charles Wentworth. (See also the Blue Mountains and the Wentworths at Homebush.) When he bought the Vaucluse estate, William kept Hayes' 1803 stone cottage as the living room of a new much larger home, completed with fittings, decorations and furnishings that were the best money could provide. The house has now been restored to its condition when occupied by the Wentworths in about 1840. A visit today is as much a celebration of the life of William Wentworth as a visit to an historic home. William Charles was one of the greats of Sydney's early colonial days, as an explorer, author, barrister and statesman, whose achievements epitomise the Australian egalitarian view that your background doesn't matter it's what you do that counts. In his role as a barrister and statesman William was instrumental in drawing up the terms of the first constitution of New South Wales, which was drafted at Vaucluse House.

William lived at Vaucluse House with his wife Sarah and children from 1827 until departing for England in 1853. When he died in England in 1872 aged 82 his body was brought back to Sydney where he was given a State funeral and his remains interred in a vault on the Vaucluse estate, now called the Wentworth Chapel, in nearby Fitzwilliam Road.

Vaucluse House is open Tuesday to Sunday 10 a.m. to 4.30 p.m. except Christmas Day and Good Friday. The house is also open public holiday Mondays.

From Vaucluse House it's a ten minute walk along Wentworth Road and Greycliffe Avenue then through Nielson Park to the sheltered harbour swimming beach at Shark Bay.

Centennial Park

Head back towards Sydney on New South Head Road and in Double Bay take Bellevue Road on the left. Follow Bellevue Road through to Old South Head Road and at Bondi Junction turn right onto the elevated expressway of Syd Einfeld Drive. From the Drive there's a good view across the rooftops of Woollahra to Sydney Harbour. At the first traffic light past the overhead pedestrian bridge turn left on York Road and after about 750 metres turn right at the entrance gates into Centennial Park.

Centennial Park is a park for all occasions. Covering 192 hectares, there are several lakes and drives, including the four kilometre long circular 'Grand Drive' with a horse track running parallel to it on the inside, avenues of palm trees and paperbark trees, groves of fir trees and a substantial rose garden. On the north side of the park a Tommaso Sani statue of a rugby player titled 'We Won' flanked by two great cannon on iron carriages captured from the Russians at Sebastopol overlooks a vista of cricket, soccer and rugby fields and the nearby park café. Not far away the Federation Pavilion houses the hexagonal granite stone which was placed under the table in England when Queen Victoria signed the Act making Australia a federation in 1901.

As you walk past the ducks, geese and black swans on the south side of Busby Lake and listen to the parrots chattering overhead in the queen and phoenix palms lining the path, you may think that the embankment seems too substantial for just a path through a park. Which it is. The path follows the route of a convict built road through Lachlan Swamps.

The site of Centennial Park was set aside as a common for grazing and watering stock by Governor Lachlan Macquarie in 1811. Between 1837-58 Lachlan Swamps were the source of Sydney's water supply through Busby's Bore providing 'soft, transparent and tasteless' (as opposed to the foul tasting Tank Stream) fresh drinking water for the citizens of Sydney. The location was the scene of a duel between Stuart Donaldson, the first Premier of New South Wales, and Thomas Mitchell, the Surveyor General. Perchance 'One More Shot Pond' at the south east corner of the park is named after the encounter.

The first suggestion that the land should become a park was made by the Governor, Lord Carrington, who was surprised that Sydney didn't have a park on the scale of those in London, Paris or New York. His idea was enthusiastically

The first Randwick Council Chambers on Avoca Street (1862) are now the St Jude's Parish Centre.

This sculpture on a window keystone kept his eye on early councillors entering the building.

High Victoriana, Randwick Lodge on Avoca Street.

supported by the Premier, Sir Henry Parkes, whose grandiose schemes for the project included an Art Gallery, Phillip Hall, where commemorative celebrations of national importance would take place, and a National Mausoleum, a kind of Westminster Abbey for Sydney reserved as a last resting place for the eminent deceased. The park never quite attained the vision Parkes had in mind, but was opened on schedule by Lord and Lady Carrington during the centenary celebrations on 26th January 1888 amid great fanfare in front of a crowd of 40,000. As relief work during the 1890s depression a band of 435 unemployed men were given work landscaping, tree planting and erecting the six kilometre long sturdy iron paling fence around the perimeter of the park. Originally there were 31 statues in the park, usually placed at the intersection of drives and paths. Not a few were maimed by out of control vehicles and some were vandalised. But a handful remain, including that of Sir Henry Parkes who gazes benevolently down on you at the fork of Parkes and Hamilton Drives.

There's a place in Sydney that whichever direction you approach it from rewards you with a little pleasing vista. Driving up the hill from the east you are greeted by the sight of the village green and the 1887 Royal Hotel with its verandah of iron lace. Approaching from the south the landscape that unfolds is the handsome Victorian stone buildings of Prince of Wales Hospital and the spire of Our Lady of the Sacred Heart church. From the west you pass the racecourse overlooked by substantial homes on Alison Road. While on this journey coming from the north along York Street and Avoca Street you pass a stone church with a square tower that looks as if its been lifted straight out of the English countryside. The place in question is, of course, Randwick.

Randwick

For Randwick's charming setting we are indebted to Simeon Pearce, who arrived in Sydney in 1842 at the age of 21 with a pound in his pocket. Pearce, who hailed from a village of weavers called Randwick in Gloucestershire, was a 'bounty immigrant' which meant he had to have secured a job in Australia before departure. In Sydney Pearce married Alice Isabella, the daughter of his employer, a wealthy ex-convict James Thompson who owned an inn at the corner of Cumberland and Essex Streets in Sydney called 'The Coach and Horses.' In September 1847 Pearce bought four acres for £20 on the so-called 'Coogee Hills' with views of Botany Bay, the Pacific Ocean, Sydney Harbour and Sydney. The following year he completed 'Blenheim House', a comfortable 10 room dwelling named after the residence of the Rector of St John's Church in Randwick, England. Appointed the local Commissioner for Crown Lands, Pearce became a prominent and wealthy land speculator through his dealings in local real estate. On his property Pearce set about building a new Randwick, not so much as a replica of the original but as a model village of comfortable homes in large grounds within easy reach of Sydney and the beaches. On the north side of the village Pearce built St Jude's 'hope of the hopeless' church as a replica of St Johns in Randwick Gloucestershire where Pearce was a bell-ringer in his youth. To the south Pearce negotiated a long-term lease of a site for a society of philanthropists who in 1856 built the Destitute Children's Asylum with dormitory accommodation for 400 inmates between the ages of four and ten. The following year Randwick's first hotel, the Coach and Horses, opened on the corner of Avoca Street and Alison Road. It also doubled for a time as Randwick's first post office, though local residents were relieved when an official post office opened, claiming 'the liquor didn't mix with the letters.'

When Randwick Municipality was incorporated in 1859 it was the first municipality in New South Wales. Simeon Pearce was elected the first Mayor at the inaugural Council meeting which took place on 1st April 1859 in a room of the Destitute Children's Asylum. Once he'd established himself Pearce invited his brother to come and live in Sydney, who married Alice Isabella's sister.

Randwick Today

The buildings of the former Destitute Children's Asylum still exist on Avoca Street as part of the Prince of Wales Hospital. Asylum inmates received daily religious instruction, while older boys were taught trades such as boot making or

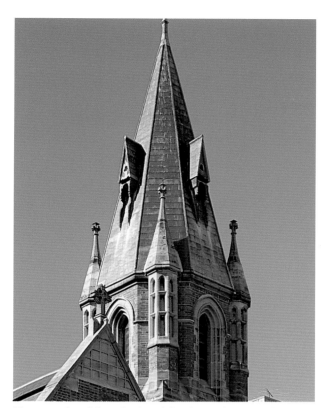

The steeple of Our Lady of the Sacred Heart Church on Avoca Street.

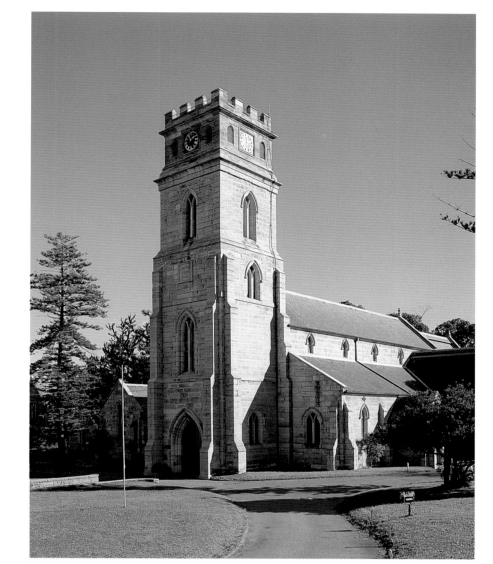

St Jude's, Randwick.

Sandstone buildings at Prince of Wales Hospital were once a destitute children's asylum.

The Royal Hotel, Randwick, during morning rush-hour.

Trucks at the Bus and Truck Museum, Tempe.

Buses at the Bus and Truck Museum, Tempe. Who could ask for more.

tailoring and girls received training in needlework, cooking and laundry duties. An early photo of the inside of the dining hall is like something straight out of Dickens, with 160 children sitting on benches at long tables lining each side of the hall. The children, with close cropped hair wearing striped uniforms are keeping still for the camera and not touching for the moment their meal served on chipped vitreous enamel plates. An overseer with a white beard wearing a black suit stands at one side with a hand resting on his lapel.

A racecourse was a fait accompli for Randwick before Randwick itself existed, maps dating from 1833 marked with an area 'Reserved for Sydney Race Course.' An early spectator recalled

> The course was through deep sand, across gullies and around hills. Occasionally the horses were lost sight of, and it was customary to bet on what horse would first reappear from behind the bank of sand which hid competitors from view.

Coming down into Randwick along Avoca Street from the north, St Jude's Church is no longer quite a replica of St John's in Gloucestershire. An extra storey was added to the top of the square tower in 1889 to accommodate a clock. It's worth spending 20 minutes visiting the old graveyard at the back of the church. You may come across the grave of Archibald Mosman after whom the Sydney suburb of Mosman is named. When Archibald sold his whaling business he retired to Coogee where he passed away peacefully in 1863 and was buried at St Jude's.

There's still a Coach and Horses Hotel on the corner of Avoca Street and Alison Road in Randwick, a mid-twentieth century structure in art deco style. A companion piece to the hotel is the old art deco 'Randwick Ritz' cinema not far away.

Another old Randwick Hotel, 'The Star and Garter Inn' faces the village green on the corner of Belmore Road and Avoca Street. The original stone building survives, though now occupied by a restaurant. The Star and Garter was Randwick's second hotel, built in the 1850s as a timber-getter's pub. In 1860 the hotel was bought by Captain Watson, Chief Sydney Harbour Pilot in the 1840s (though no relation of Watson of Watsons Bay) who converted the hotel to a house and added the square tower to the building. Watson also commissioned the statue of Captain Cook which stands on the street outside facing Botany Bay.

Simeon Pearce's stone home 'Blenheim House' still stands at 17 Blenheim Street, but he'd cry if he saw it today. Though the house itself has been restored it's sandwiched between two blocks of flats, the one on the west side rudely blocking the view not four meters from its verandah.

Tempe Bus and Truck Museum

Head west out of Randwick past the racecourse on Alison Road and along Dacey Avenue, McEvoy Street and Mitchell Road to the Princes Highway, then turn left to reach after about three kilometres, Tempe. The Bus and Truck Museum is on Gannon Street, a one-way street which you can't turn on to from the Princes Highway so you need to approach by Unwins Bridge Road and Griffiths Street.

Tempe Bus and Truck Museum was founded by a group of enthusiasts from the Historic Commercial Vehicle Association in the old Tempe tramsheds in 1986. Many of the vehicles on display are the only remaining examples of their type left in Australia. There are about 80 buses in the museum, 50 of which are in working order and 25 are licensed for road use and carrying passengers. Exhibits range from an early 'Ruggles' 1924 bus to the 1970s Atlantean's which were the last double-deckers to operate on Sydney's roads. The museum, which is open Wednesdays 10 a.m. to 3 p.m. and Sundays from 10 a.m. to 4 p.m. also has a smaller collection of trucks. Purchase of an entry ticket on Sundays includes unlimited rides on a vintage double-decker bus which leaves the museum for a half-hour sightseeing tour of 'cosmopolitan' Newtown at 15 minutes past the hour every hour between 10.15 am. and 3.15 p.m.

Sydney Tramway Museum

Travelling another 20 kilometres south on the Princes Highway to Loftus an unusual structure on the right with a pagoda like top marks the location of

Sydney Tramway Museum. The pagoda was a tram signal box which stood for many years on top of the tram shelter on Railway Square outside Central Railway Station. The entire structure was moved to its present location in 1991 and is now a shelter for the adjoining picnic area at the museum.

Sydney Tramway Museum, entry to which is on Pitt Street off Rawson Avenue, takes you on a nostalgic journey through the history of Sydney's trams, which operated for 100 years from 1861 to 1961. In days gone by a fleet of 1,400 trams ran along 180 miles of route providing Sydney with a network that had twice as many trams as Melbourne has today. In the display hall are over 50 trams, many in working order, others under restoration, mostly from Sydney and Australia but including examples from San Francisco, Berlin, Nagasaki and Milan.

A tram from the Tramway Museum on its regular outing to the stop in Royal National Park.

A beautifully restored exhibit is 'No. 290', a fully functional 1896 tram which is the oldest example in existence of an electric tram built in Australia. Nearby stands 'Sydney Scrubber No. 134S' a tram fitted with a special device that cleaned the rails as the tram ran along the track. When it was pressed into service again recently to clean the rails of Sydney's new light rail before it went into service at Darling harbour many people thought the strange contraption was one of Sydney's new trams. Last, but not least, mention must be made of 'Prison Tram No.948' used to carry up to 24 inmates between Darlinghurst Courthouse and Long Bay Gaol in six compartments, four for men and two for women. The tram ran off a spur on the La Perouse line to a terminus inside the main gate of Long Bay. There was only one escape from the tram, in 1946, when 25 year old Darcy Dugan and a fellow inmate cut through the coachwood roof with a breadknife on the way from Darlinghurst to Long Bay and ran into Centennial Park. Listed are the names of seven prisoners who weren't quite so lucky. The tram journey was the last they ever made for they were taken from the court to Long Bay to be hanged for murder.

The museum is open on Sundays and Public Holidays from 10 a.m. until 5 p.m. and on Wednesdays from 9.30 a.m. until 3.30 p.m. Included in the entry fee is a return two kilometre tram ride through the bush to Royal National Park Tram Terminus.

The beautifully restored interior of 'No 290', the oldest tram in Australia. Wedges on the seats were to prevent passengers sliding into one another under braking.

Royal National Park

Heavy seas pound the wild coastline of Royal National Park. Little Marley Beach is in the foreground, Marley Beach in the distance.

Royal National Park

The bird-life is just one of the attractions of Royal National Park. You are more than likely to see one of these cheeky characters on a visit to the park, a sulphur-crested cockatoo.

Royal National Park has the distinction of being the oldest national park in the world, formed on 26th April 1879. Yellowstone Park in the U.S.A. was founded earlier in 1872, but it wasn't named as a national park until 1883. Sydney's National Park became the Royal following the visit of Queen Elizabeth in 1954. Since 1967 the park has been administered by the National Parks and Wildlife Service.

Royal National Park, receiving over a million visitors a year, is the most visited national park in Australia. Its sloping sandstone plateau of over 15,000 hectares includes rugged, high sandstone cliffs and surfing beaches, extensive heathlands, subtropical rainforest vegetation in the creek gullies, tall eucalypt forests on the drier slopes and more open woodland and bush on the high ground. This landscape is traversed by over 150 kilometres of bush walking tracks. There are shaded picnic and barbecue areas at Audley with boats available for hire on the freshwater lake in the valley.

If travelling to the south coast and you're not in a hurry it is worth making a diversion through the national park. The turnoff on Farnell Road near Loftus is 29 kilometres from Sydney's G.P.O. The Visitor Centre a few hundred metres on the left provides maps and information on the park. There's road access to Bundeena, Wattamolla and Garie Beach. The route along Sir Bertram Stevens Drive, Lady Wakehurst Drive and Otford Road takes you back to the highway, or a scenic 28 kilometre drive along the coast through Coalcliff, Coledale, Thirroul and Bulli takes you to Wollongong. The main roads through Royal National Park to Audley, Bundeena, Waterfall and Otford stay open 24 hours, but minor roads to the beaches and into the bush are closed by a locked gate 8.30 at night.

The main southern railway line runs close to the western boundary of the park, so it's a short walk for rail travellers to enter the park from stations at Loftus, Engadine, Heathcote, Waterfall or Otford. Royal National Park is also easily accessible from Sydney's southern suburbs, The McKell Avenue road entrance to the park at Waterfall is 33 kilometres from Liverpool.

History of Royal National Park

For the existence of the park we are indebted to the Premier Sir John Robertson who believed

> Cities, towns and villages should be possessed of pleasure grounds as places of recreation to ensure the sound health and vigour of the community...

> This immense people's reserve ... [would be] suitable for military manoeuvres, recreation and camping grounds, or for plantations of ornamental trees and shrubs.

For this place of recreation 'sections in the parishes of Sutherland, Heathcote and Bulgo, and the whole of the Crown lands within the parish of Wattamolla' were reserved from sale and on 26th April 1879 dedicated for 'the use of the public forever as a national park'. Fortunately one of the park's greatest assets, the Hacking River valley, remained in a near pristine state frequented by the odd fisherman or woodcutter because it had been set aside as a possible route for the Illawarra Railway. The care of the park was vested with a group of trustees with Sir John Robertson the first President of the National Park Trust. The original reserve of 7,300 hectares was expanded to 14,700 hectares in 1880 and small areas added since have brought the total area of the park to approximately 16,000 hectares.

In Port Hacking fishing was a major activity in the 1880s with 512 fishermen and 236 fishing boats licensed to operate there from the Georges River, Botany Bay and Sydney. Sir Henry Parkes didn't endear himself to the fishermen when in 1886 he banned netting in Port Hacking to ensure there were adequate fish stocks for line fishing in the National Park. Pockets of privately owned land still existing on the south shore of Port Hacking such as at Carruther's Bay and Gogerly's Point date back to old land grants.

By-laws were introduced by the park trustees to, for example, put a stop to the 'modern abomination of advertising on rocks and trees... Here at least Nature's beauties can be enjoyed without notifications concerning So-and-So's soap, or Somebody's

Embrocation, or Otherman's Pills vulgarising everything.' In 1902 there were still dingoes in the park but the trustees believed it was not their place 'to nurture or foster the growth of these pests.'

Audley

The first area developed in the park was close to the tidal limit of the Hacking River, where visitors could be landed off by shallow draught vessel from Sydney. The place was named Audley after the surveyor Lord Audley who in 1864 made a detailed survey of the river. His camp was near the junction of the Hacking River and Kangaroo Creek. Lord Audley's wife Emily, whom he married in 1857, was a daughter of the Surveyor-General, Sir Thomas Mitchell. Land was cleared for a horse paddock, a fruit and vegetable garden and a pavilion. With the building of a dam across the river the valley at the junction of Kangaroo Creek and the Hacking River was transformed into a Y-shaped lake for boating and a sturdy wooden boatshed was built on the shore.

A spur off the Southern Railway to National Park Station completed in 1886 terminated on the plateau just 25 minutes walk from Audley or a quick trip down the hill by horse and buggy. Also completed in 1886 was Lady Carrington Drive winding through the Hacking River Valley. Advertised in contemporary literature on the park as 'the most beautiful drive in the world' visitors could explore its delights on horseback or by horse-drawn sulky. By 1893 Audley had a dining room, apartments and sleeping accommodation for 22 guests, a slip and shed for hauling and repairing boats, a blacksmith's shop, carpenter's shops and stables.

An 'attractive improvement' made to the park in 1885 was the clearing of 65 hectares along the shore of Port Hacking for a deer park enclosed by a 1.8 metre high fence. Over the following years the enclosure was stocked with fallow deer from Parramatta Park, red deer gifted by E. S. Cox, a descendant of William Cox of Blue Mountains fame and Sambar deer from the then Dutch East Indies. At various times the deer broke out of the enclosure and escaped into the National Park, where finding the environment to their liking they bred like rabbits. There are now estimated to be hundreds of wild deer roaming the park, the most hardy and most common have proved to be the Javan rusas.

Loftus

An area near the north west entry to the park, on the railway line, was called Loftus Heights after the Governor of New South Wales, Lord Augustus William Frederick Spencer Loftus.

Lady Wakehurst Drive, which enters Royal National Park near Otford, cuts through dense forest country.

Cabbage tree palm forest on The McKell Avenue. Singed trunks are a legacy of the 1994 bush fires.

The extraordinary form of an angophora tree growing close to the roadside at Audley.

Governor from August 1879 to November 1885 and hailing from Clifton, Bristol in the U.K., Loftus was the British Ambassador in Berlin during the Austro-Prussian and Franco-German wars and before coming to N.S.W. had been the Ambassador to Russia in St Petersburg. His posting to Sydney was after a request for a less taxing appointment in a warmer climate. The opening of the railway heralded the start of military manoeuvres at Loftus on 800 hectares cleared of 'wild scrub'. An annual Easter Encampment held from 1886 to 1901 was attended by 'our infantry, mounted infantry, cavalry and field artillery forces'. Thirty thousand visitors travelled from Sydney by train to watch the first army manoeuvres from Loftus in 1886. Flagstaff Hill was used to send signals by heliograph to defensive positions in Sydney such as Middle Head, South Head and Bare Island. Farnell Avenue leading into the park off the Princes Highway was originally built by the army to haul field guns across the park, over the lower causeway at Audley and up to 'Artillery Hill Camp' on the other side. The camp was used as a firing range to pound the countryside in the direction of the coast with explosive shells. Shrapnel Hill and Shrapnel Hill Trail near the Bundeena turn-off of Bertram Stevens Drive commemorate the phenomenon. Artillery Hill Camp was used as a firing range until the start of the First World War.

Damage wrought to the bush landscape by shellfire was as nothing compared to the total devastation of this section of the park by the 1994 bushfires. Twelve thousand hectares, fully three quarters of the park's surface, was burnt-out or damaged by the fires leaving kilometre after kilometre of nothing but sandy soil with a grey coating of ash. Aerial photos of the park taken at this time on display in the Visitor Centre resemble a lunar landscape. Remarkably, the bush has come back, though it is likely to be generations before the park regains something of its former equilibrium. All the photos of the park in this book were taken in the last two or three years, so things aren't quite as bad as they may seem.

Lady Carrington Walk

I've enjoyed every walk I've been on in the Royal National Park, but there are three in particular I've reserved for a mention here because between them they cover the most spectacular scenery in the park. The first is Lady Carrington Walk, completed in 1886 and opened by Lady Carrington, wife of Baron Carrington, Governor of N.S.W. originally called 'Lady Carrington Road', renamed 'Lady Carrington Drive' in 1916 and now known as 'Lady Carrington Walk'. Since being closed to traffic, the walk can be done from Audley or from just above the junction of McKell Avenue on Sir Bertram Stevens Drive where it is signposted opposite the remains of an old shale quarry. From the entry at Audley it is 9.6 kilometres to the end of the walk on Sir Bertram Stevens Drive. It's a comfortable one-way three hour walk if you have two cars and can leave one at the other end or an easy three hour two-way trip by bicycle.

Sea mist blowing-in over the coast of the Royal National Park.

Dry stone walls by the roadside are part of the scenery at Audley.

These exotic fir trees at Audley date to the time this section of the park was first developed for the public.

Visitors to Audley pass the time in the same way as they have for 150 years, with picnics and boating. The only difference is that now they arrive by car instead of train and ship.

Another view of Uloola Falls.

Looking towards National Falls.

Uloola Falls cascades over a low cliff by two terraces.

Birdlife

The early trustees used Aboriginal bird names to identify the 15 'brooks' crossed by the road, including Burunda Brook (swan), Karaga Brook (white crane) and Dirinjiri Brook (wagtail). Over 200 species of birds have been identified in Royal National Park and you're certain to see at least half a dozen of them on the trek through Lady Carrington Walk. The raucous alarm cry of cheeky sulphur-crested cockatoos fills the air as a flock wings over the tree canopy like a squadron of forest guardians on a mission. You may be startled by the sudden red and blue flash of a crimson rosella darting across the road, which can be particularly unnerving at nesting time when they'll make a bee-line straight for your head at lightning speed then turn at the last moment to skim just over your hair. Other birds are more likely to be heard than seen such as the distinctive whooping crack of the eastern whipbird or the loud clapping noise as a wonga pigeon takes flight.

A small cascade above Uloola Falls.

From Audley the walk follows the course of the Hacking River through a winding steep-sided wooded valley. The old drive undulates slightly on the way, so is sometimes close to inviting grassy picnic stops on the riverbank and at others perched halfway up the valley with a view looking down through the trees to the Hacking River flashing in the sunlight. Quite a variety of trees cling to the valley sides. At the start of the walk the thick, strange writhing forms of orange angophora trees hold sway but these give way to majestic blue gums, blackbutts and turpentine trees, their lines of soaring trunks often broken by a splash of green from the curling fronds of cabbage tree palms. The Aborigines used to use the leaves of the cabbage tree palms as a wrapping when collecting seeds.

A good spot for a picnic before turning back, if doing the walk from one direction, is the Calala clearing about half-way between Audley and Sir Bertram Stevens Drive. In the centre of the clearing surrounded by Australian bush stands a thriving English oak tree. As you eat your picnic beneath the shade of its branches you can pretend you are Robin Hood in Sherwood Forest. You probably won't see the Sheriff of Nottingham, but may spy the Park Ranger on the road in his four-wheel drive. He won't let you pick the wildflowers but may not mind if you're grilling venison on the barbecue – deer aren't part of the native Australian fauna.

The Forest Path

The west bank of Bola Creek just past the bridge on Lady Carrington Walk, or the carpark at the end of Lady Carrington Walk on Sir Bertram Stevens Drive, is the starting point for 'The Forest Path'. A circular track just over five kilometres long, the path was originally completed in 1886 not long after the opening of Lady Carrington Road. Land surveyors

A small falls near the road above the Forest Path.

Birds Nest ferns on the Forest Path.

The Forest Path.

Previous pages: National Falls are just off The McKell Avenue which leads into the park from Waterfall.

The wilderness in the upper reaches of Bola Gully.

who had discovered the jungle-like vegetation along the upper Hacking River and its tributary Bola Creek reckoned 'no forest within 100 miles of Sydney was comparable to it' and the track was cleared through the undergrowth 'to afford convenient access to the finest forest trees'. Over the years the track became overgrown and disused and was rebuilt in 1988 as a Bicentennial project. Sections of the west portion of the track damaged in the 1994 bush fires were recovering well when I went through in 1998.

A shameful man-made degradation took place in the 1920s when the Park Trust gave a coal company permission to log timber from the Hacking River Valley area in return for the payment of a royalty. Logging activities commenced and a sawmill was built in a gully near the Upper Causeway. The subsequent campaign mounted in the press was one of the first triumphs by conservationists in halting the logging of native forests. A September 1922 report in the *Sydney Morning Herald* brought the public attention to the landscape of hundreds of ugly tree stumps and piles of dead trees left by the timber cutters. However the Trust wasn't prepared to budge, dismissing the criticism as that of 'cranks and fanatics'. It was the Minister for Lands who intervened a week after the article was published, informing the Trust they must cancel the contract. In consequence the Trust had to pay back the coal company royalties of £1562 plus legal costs.

This isn't a walk to be hurried, allow two hours so there's plenty of time to enjoy the rainforest scenery along the way. Above the south side of Bola Creek bridge the Wallumarra Track follows the banks of Bola Creek through the rainforest to Bola Gully offering a further avenue for exploration. The Wallumarra Track continues up the hill to Sir Bertram Stevens Drive on Black Gin Ridge.

Lady Carrington Drive.

Rainforest

Heading east (left) from the start of the path on Sir Bertram Stevens Drive, twenty minutes walk brings you to the rainforest scenery on the Hacking River. Twenty five species of rainforest climbers and over 50 species of rainforest trees have been recorded in the Hacking River and Bola Creek area. The reason they thrive here is because the local Narrabeen shales weather into a much richer clay soil than the poorer sandstone soils predominating in the rest of the park. Along the track the dense canopy shades a real wilderness of delicate ferns, sinuously curling vines and colourful fungi and toadstools erupting from rotting boughs on the forest floor. An occasional rock coated with moss and lichens sprouts a creamy bloom of tiny rock orchids which seem too delicate to survive in this primeval landscape.

Even here there's birdlife. You may experience the thrill of seeing a male lyrebird with its magnificent plume of tail feathers, scratching about in the undergrowth searching for grubs. The National Parks and Wildlife Service uses the male lyrebird on its logo. In the more open patches of forest a common sight is the crow-like satin bowerbird, the sunlight bouncing with a semi-gloss indigo sheen off its coat as it filters through the trees.

Near the junction with Lady Carrington Walk several of the most gigantic rainforest trees provide shelter for some benches and picnic tables. Fifteen minutes walk to the right on Lady Carrington Drive takes you back to the car.

The Coast Track

For an enjoyable weekend away from it all, close to Sydney, take a trek on The Coast Track. The walk can be comfortably done in two days allowing for stops and sight-seeing on the way, and covers a total distance of about 30 kilometres along the coast of Royal National Park from Bundeena in the north almost to the park's southern boundary at Otford Lookout. It's one of the best walks around Sydney, also quite popular, so certainly at the weekend you won't be alone making this trek. If using public transport access is straightforward by train to Cronulla and ferry to Bundeena then train from Otford Station to return to Sydney. If going by car it's useful if you can arrange to leave a vehicle at Wattamolla with most of the food and camping gear from where it's a twenty minute walk to a bush camp-site at Curracurrang Gully. Long trousers are more comfortable because the coastal heath growing close to the path for much of the route has sharp spiky leaves. Camping permits should be obtained beforehand from the Visitor Centre near Audley.

Bundeena

For most of its life Bundeena has been an island community accessible only by boat. The first land grant known as the 'Yarmouth Estate' was of 400 acres to Owen Byrne in 1823. In 1863 an employee of Thomas Holt, George Simpson, bought 50 acres of the estate at

Primeval landscape on the Forest Path.

Cabbage Tree Point and his son built a large house known as 'Simpson's Hotel' which became a popular honeymooner's retreat. The Ranger's lodge is built on the house foundations. Simpson Road and Simpsons Bay are reminders of the first recreation destination on the south shore of Port Hacking.

A short cut to the coast track is from the locked gate at the end of Beachcomber Avenue, however if you wish to be pedantic and boast that you've walked all the way I'm afraid you'll have to start by heading east out of Bundeena on Loftus Street. If taking the latter option, follow The Avenue and Lambeth Walk past Gunyah Beach. In 1934 lots with 'absolute water frontages' on Gunyah Beach were auctioned with £3 deposit down and repayment of £1 per month at 5% interest. Continue on Neil Street to Jibbon Beach. A track behind the beach passes Jibbon Lagoons to join the Coast Track. Just off the coast the waves break on Jibbon Bombora, the scene of a tragedy when a ship called the *Nemesis* struck the rocks and sank on 9th July 1904.

If starting the walk at Beachcomber Avenue, a sandy path leads through the heath to the track. This hardy coastal heath growing on thin sandy soil seems to flourish in the tough cliff-top environment of buffeting winds and salt-spray. No less than 700 species of flowering plants were found in this heathland though inevitably this number must have declined since the bushfires wreaked havoc in the area. Even so the heath has fought back and now once more coats the cliff tops. In spring the landscape is coloured by the tiny pink, white, red and mauve flowers of the heath, adding a subtle shade to the bright yellow glow of the wattles. Many species of birds frequent the heath, some of them permanent residents, others migratory visitors. Honeyeaters darting among the bushes are one of the permanents. An occasional albatross has been spotted off the cliffs, gliding his way north from the southern oceans.

Marley

On Marley Head the elements have sculpted the coloured sandstone into all sorts of beautiful shapes. Traces of iron or manganese in the compacted white quartz granules forming the sandstone make burgundy or yellow lines through the rock.

From the top of Marley Head there's a view of the unspoilt expanse of Big Marley Beach and its baby brother, Little Marley. Black swans sometimes frequent Marley Lagoon behind Big Marley Beach. Big Marley Beach incidentally is considered dangerous for swimming. The grassy flat backing onto Little Marley Beach is popular for bush camping. Fresh water is available from a small stream, though to be on the safe side it is recommended that no creek water in the park should be drunk untreated. A grove of cabbage tree palms at the rear of the grassy flat was singed by the 1994 bushfires but seems to have sprung back to life.

The track above Bola Creek.

Lush under-storey of ferns and palms on the Forest Path.

A tributary on Bola Creek.

Horderns Beach and Jibbon Beach form the southern boundary of Port Hacking. The diminutive Cronulla ferry cuts across the turquoise waters of Port Hacking at the centre of the picture.

Horderns Beach, Bundeena.

The Cronulla-Bundeena ferry off Bundeena.

Wattamolla

After crossing the cliff tops south of Marley, the track drops down to Wattamolla at the creek above Wattamolla Lagoon. Children swimming in fresh water Wattamolla Lagoon seem determined to ignore the notice on a high rock next to the track warning against jumping into the lagoon because of the risk of spinal injury. Wattamolla, with its beach, lagoon, cleared grassy paddocks and plentiful car parking space is a popular destination for weekend family outgoings. A kiosk is open at weekends. The beach was originally named Providential Cove because Bass, Flinders and Boy Martin sheltered out a storm here in March 1797 during their Port Hacking venture. The aboriginal name for the beach endured, but Providential Head on the north side of the cover and Boy Martin Point Lookout on the south side commemorate Flinder's visit. Wattamolla was in the news the following year when in 1797 three survivors of the *Sydney Cove* shipwreck were rescued at the beach after they lit a signal fire from lumps of foraged coal. In an extraordinary epic of survival after struggling ashore from the wrecked ship in Bass Strait they had walked all the way from Victoria.

Bush scenery on Sir Bertram Stevens Drive.

Curracurrang

Twenty minutes walk from Wattamolla on the south side of Curracurrang Gully there's some space for camping on small flat grassy clearings surrounded by bush. It is locations like this where at dusk you may see one of the swamp wallabies or red-necked wallabies that frequent the park. A further 40 minutes or so south of the gully there's a view from the track of Eagle Rock, a formation like an eagle's head jutting from the cliff top. Nearby, Curracurrong Creek drops from the top of the cliff to the sea by a waterfall. When I passed there was a strong southerly blowing and the waterfall was transformed by the wind into a moving curtain of water that was blown back over the cliffs before it could hit the rocks.

Karloo Pool, a deep freshwater swimming pool, is accessed by the Karloo Track leading down from Heathcote.

Garie

From the top of Garie North Head there's a spectacular view extending to Wollongong and Port Kembla. Garie Beach below is named after an Aboriginal word for 'sleepy'. The beach woke up from its sleep in the late nineteenth century when a local reported a rich alluvial gold find in one of the creeks, backed up by the authentication of a sample by the Department of Mines. But prospectors who joined the subsequent gold rush couldn't find a trace and the man in question bolted before they could get their vengeful hands on him. Parcels of land at Garie were granted to early settlers in the 1830s, who cleared it for grazing. Garie Beach and the surrounding countryside became part of the National Park in 1934. The road to Garie as well as some of the other roads in the park were built by out of work men paid by Unemployment Relief funds during the depression of the 1930s. There's a car park and weekend kiosk at Garie, also a Youth Hostel.

Trekking across Garie Beach then rounding Thelma Head you reach North and South

Lady Wakehurst Drive.

Bush-walkers on the Coast Track, heading north towards Little Marley Beach.

Wattamolla Beach.

A strong southerly blows the waters of Curracurrong Creek straight back up the cliff to form a perpetual waterfall.

A swimmer at Wattamolla about to disobey the sign warning against jumping or diving into the lagoon. People have broken their necks here.

213

Earthy colours on a tree trunk on the Coast Track not far from Otford.

Era beaches which were also once privately owned. It's not hard to imagine that land cleared in the area was once used for grazing cattle. After farmers gave up commercial farming they didn't have the heart to slaughter all their stock and for years afterwards wild cattle roamed the slopes. A feature called Stockyard Gully at North Era is a reminder of the time Era was farming country. On the slopes near South Era Beach and in the Burning Palms area are about 100 shack-like homes held on permissive occupancy. The only access to the huts is by foot, but the residents seem happy enough with their isolated pioneer-like existence. The cleared slopes around Era are favourite grazing pastures for Royal National Park's deer and its not unusual to see small herds or individuals in the vicinity.

Burning Palms

Burning Palms Beach south of Era was named by an early conservationist Myles Dunphy after the lighting of a bonfire of dry cabbage tree fronds at night for a beacon. Dunphy was a founding member of the Mountain Trails Club, and it was the lobbying of this club and the Sydney Bushwalker's Club of the Government that were instrumental in securing Era and Burning Palms for the National Park in 1945.

About 15 minutes south of Burning Palms Beach the track starts to climb the escarpment on a carpet of fallen palm leaves through the 'Palm Jungle', a forest of cabbage tree and bangalay palms interspersed with rainforest trees draped with hanging vines. It's a stiff climb to the cliff top 200 metres above then about 25 minutes walk through attractive bushland to the road at Otford Lookout. Werrong Beach, an authorised nude bathing beach backed by littoral rainforest, is accessed by a steep path on the left. From Otford Lookout it's five minutes or so walk to Otford Station.

The Coast Track on the heights above Garie Beach.

The Coast Track near Otford Lookout.

Burning Palms Beach.

North and South Era beaches. The light area on North Era Beach closest to the camera is a giant Aboriginal midden.

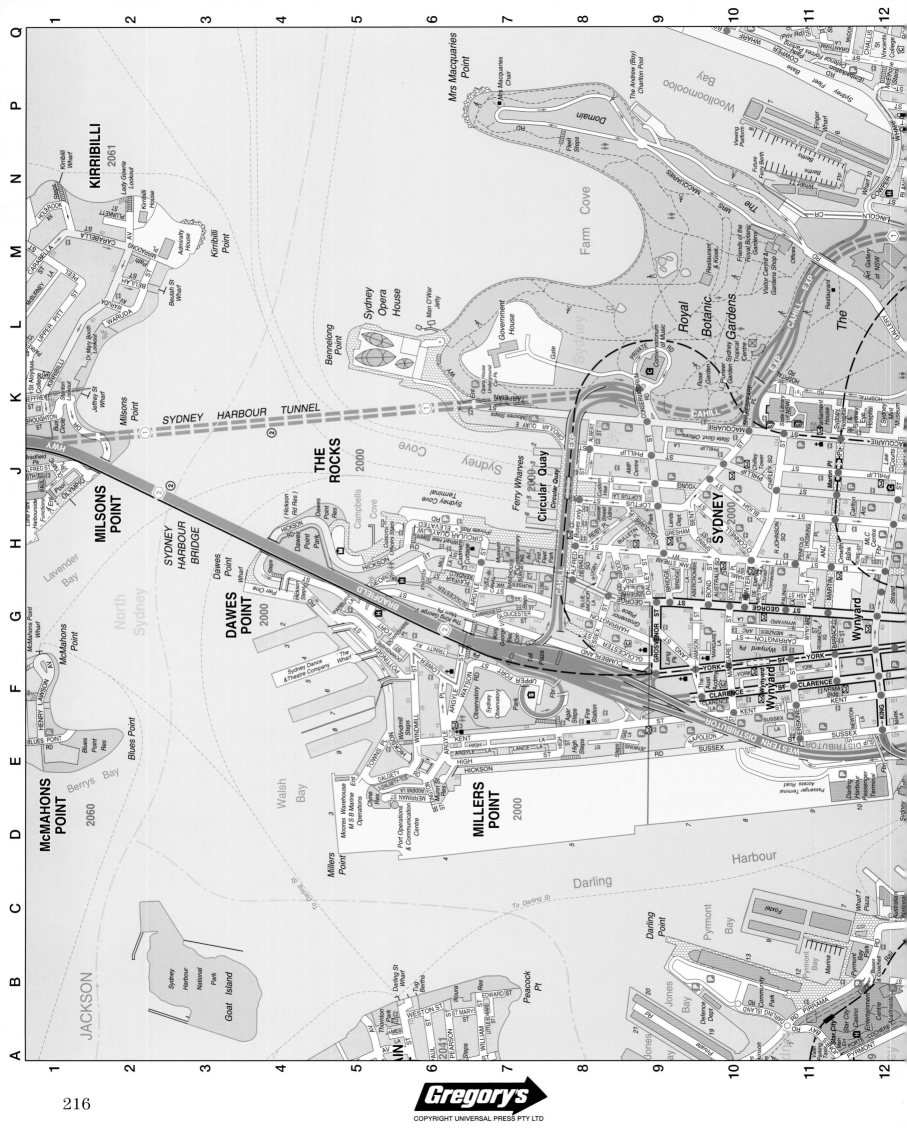

217

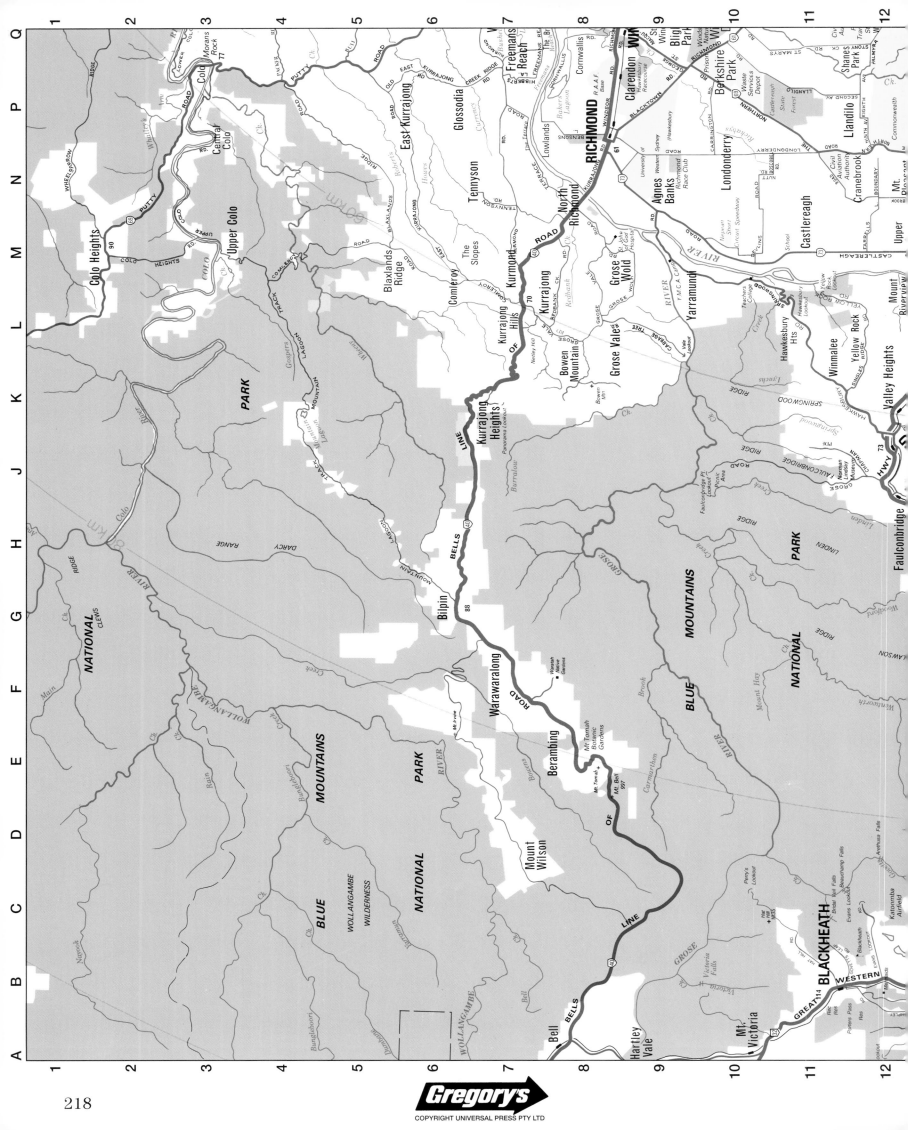

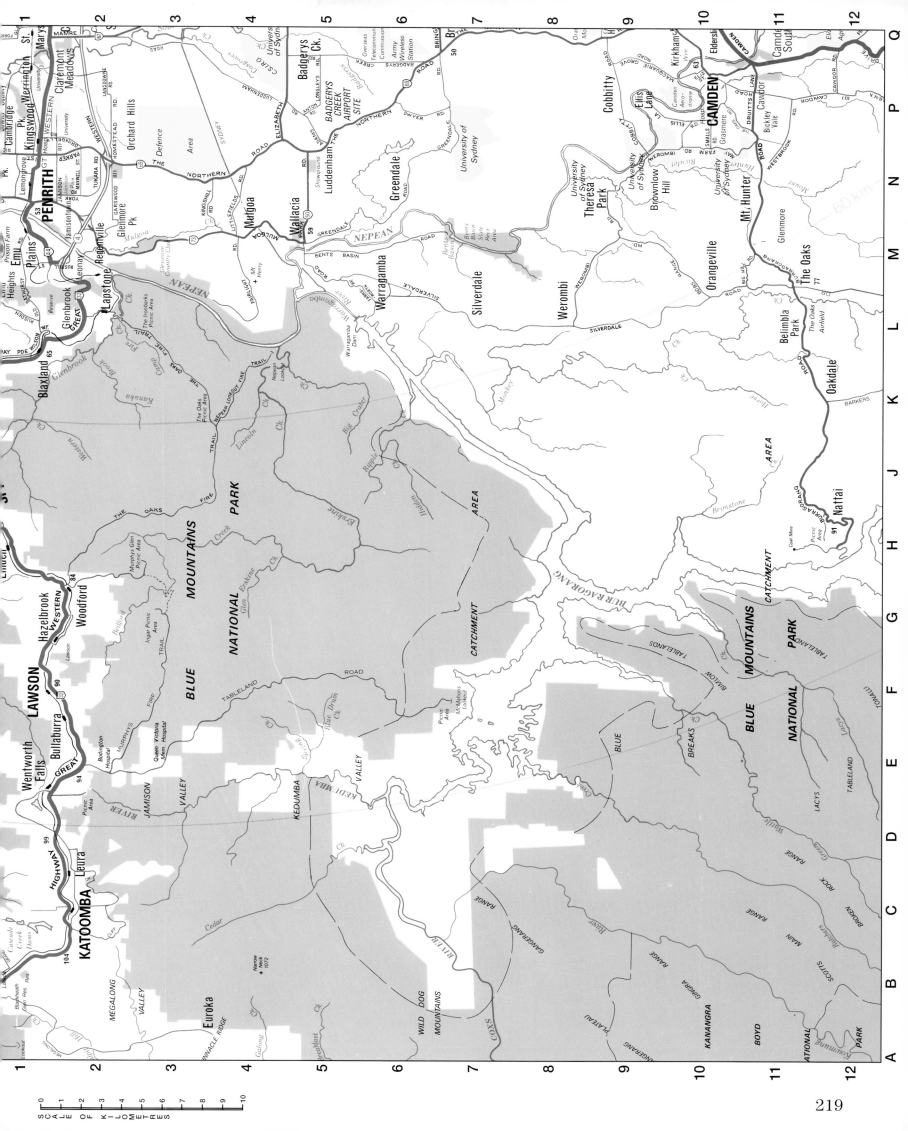

219

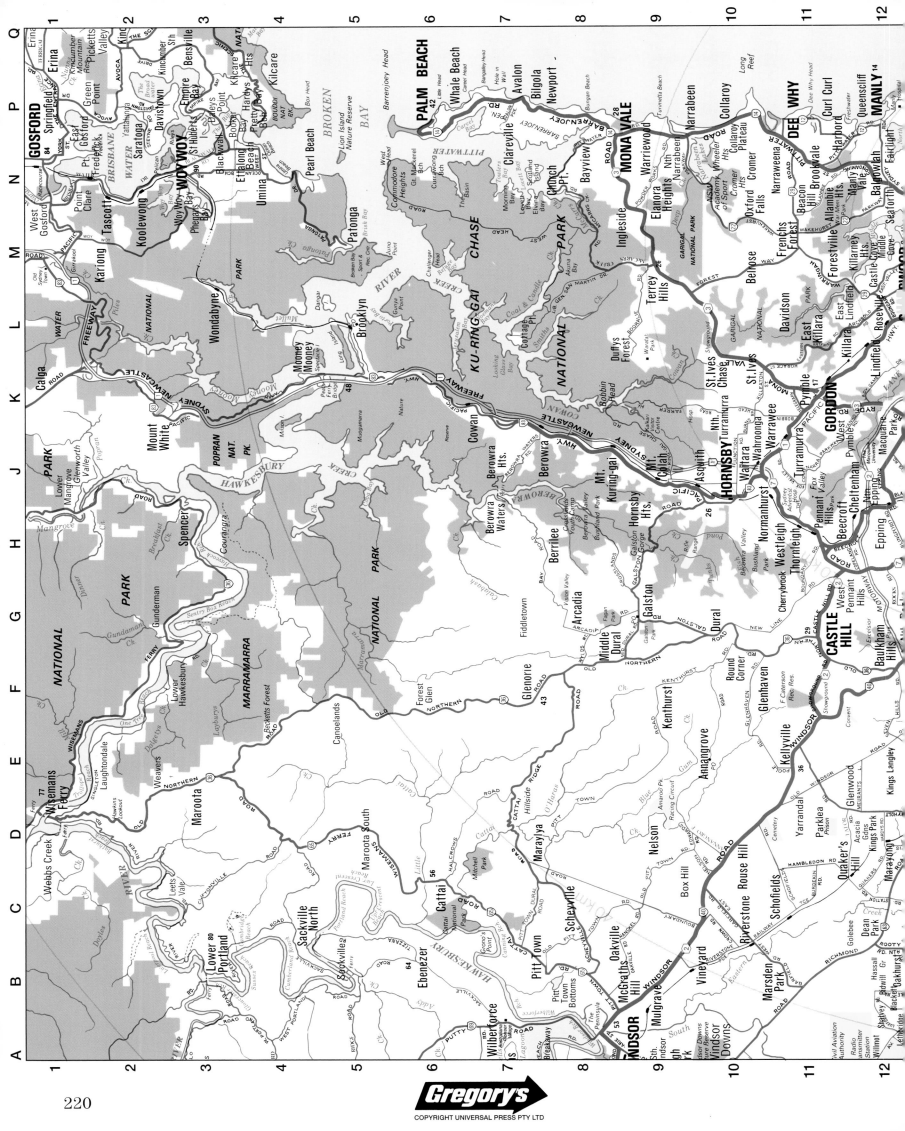

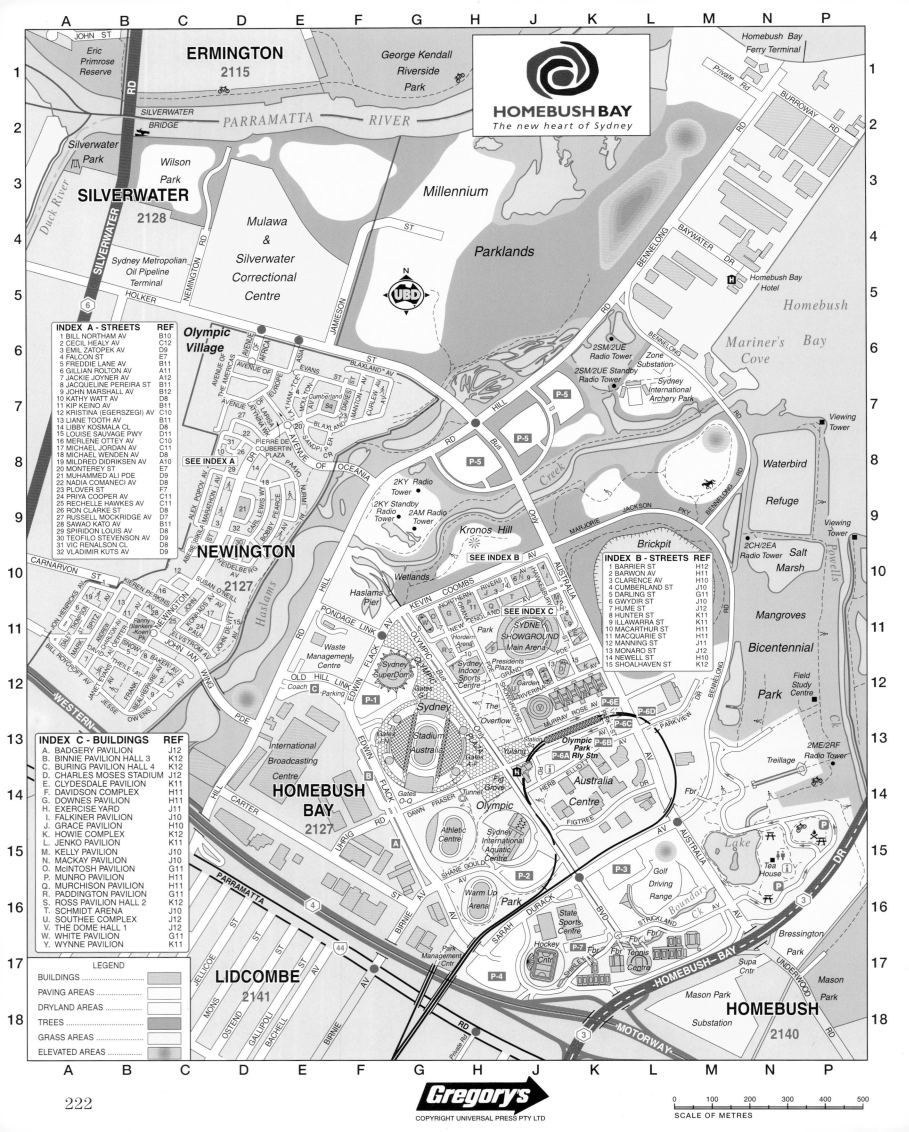

Index

References in parentheses refer to maps.